Dance
for Young Children
Finding the Magic
in Movement

Sue Stinson

D1301088

Sponsored by the National Dance Association
an association of the
American Alliance for Health, Physical Education, Recreation, and Dance

Third printing 1993
copyright ©1988

The American Alliance for
Health, Physical Education,
Recreation, and Dance
1900 Association Dr.
Reston, Virginia 22091
ISBN 0-88314-381-X

To Chelle and Ben,
who taught me most

Contents

v

Introduction

There exists in each of us a desire to achieve—to know more and do more. We want to run, jump, and fly, and then go farther and faster. This drive has generated many individual and societal accomplishments of which we are justly proud. Human knowledge has increased dramatically and continues to increase by geometric proportions. We have made a complex world in which there is much to know and do, enough challenges to last several lifetimes. This part of ourselves lends excitement to our lives and stimulates us to move beyond where we are.

At the same time, this desire generates conflicts for us, because our lives often seem *too* busy. There is far more to get done in a day, a week, or a year than there is time in which to do it, and we seem always in ahurry to finish the present task in order to move on to the next one. Today, educators seem particularly faced with this dilemma: As there is more and more that people need to know, how will there be time for teaching—and learning—it all? Teachers of young children struggle with an increasing demand for teaching their students the "basic academic skills" at an earlier and earlier age, and parents struggle with how to schedule all of the activities that seem necessary for their children to become accomplished and productive individuals. Even preschoolers seem rushed at times, as they insistently ask us *"when* can I . . . ?" or "How many more minutes until . . . ?"

Despite the strength of this drive, we also possess its opposite—a desire to stop trying to get somewhere and appreciate where we are *right now*. In this dimension, we pay attention not so much to *where* we are going as to *how* we are getting there. This happens, for example, when we stop trying to get dinner over with in order to accomplish the evening chores, and instead appreciate the tastes and textures of our food, allowing mealtime to become a sensory experience. When we pay so much attention to the familiar, it often becomes strange for us, rather like a super-enlarged photograph of grains of salt that reveals a crystal garden. At such moments, we feel as though we have stepped outside everyday time and space, or even entered another world. We know ourselves and our world in a different and deeper way. We may even imagine new identities for ourselves, or new worlds we might enter.

Preschool children seem to have special access to this other reality. Anyone who has tried to get somewhere with a young child knows that these children have an uncanny way of not only slowing us down, but also helping us notice things along the way that we might otherwise miss—the procession of ants down the sidewalk, the importance of a hug *right now*, even the sound of grass growing. I cherish young children for leading me into this world with them, for helping me find this part of myself that all too often gets ignored in the busy-ness of my life.

Artists treasure this other reality into which young children enter so readily, because it is where the creative spirit lives. Indeed, the arts offer another way to get in touch with deeper parts of ourselves and a deeper awareness of the world. Some adults even speak of how participating in the arts helps them find the child within themselves.

Of all the arts, dance is the form in which I have found a "home." While in everyday life I just *use* my body, in dance I sense it in a different way. I become aware of much that I otherwise take for granted, such as what a stretch feels like, or how I use my feet to get into the air in a jump. Further, I become more attuned to other forms and other movements that exist in the world—the energy of a crowd of children entering a room, patterns of light and shadow, pathways of leaves falling to earth.

Yet, dance also satisfies a need I share with young children—the need to *MOVE* . . . to run, jump, and even fly. It speaks to my desire for challenge and excitement and achievement as well as calmness and centering.

Being a teacher has given me an opportunity to combine my love for children and my love for dance. Of course, I found out quickly that love, while essential for teaching, is not enough. Some very important knowledge and a lot of hard work are also necessary if one is to create a vision, whether that vision is an artistic or an educational one.

As our visions grow, so do we as teachers. I used to think of a teacher as a finished product in the business of learning, the perfect (or nearly so) model to whom the student would aspire. Now I recognize the inaccuracy of this view, especially in the creative arts. As a teacher, I first must share a part of myself, creating a space in which children are free to discover and share a part of themselves. In the process, we both learn more about ourselves and each other. We do not have a preconceived notion of just how we will "end up," but are constantly in the process of *becoming*. Children have the space to become, not just like the teacher, but more fully themselves.

Each teacher will also develop differently, with an individual style of teaching, based on unique experiences and the special gift of who he or she is as a person. The teacher does not need to be perfect, but has the right to try new ideas, and also to fail, in the process of growth. Seeing this kind of openness also gives children the freedom to risk themselves in the learning process.

This book is meant to be a part of the growth process for you, the teacher. It will not by itself make anyone a master teacher of dance; that requires extensive experience in the art. Learning in any of the arts demands more than just reading and thinking. Even this book requires more than passive reading if it is going to make a contribution to you and your classroom. You will need to feel movement in your own body as you read about movement, to find other examples when some are given, and to imagine the responses of your own class as you plan a session. My ideas may get you started, but you will need to adapt them to your own situation and then generate your own ideas. This is a large order but, as all teachers of preschool children know, great investments of our own energy yield rich returns.

The first chapter of the book will give you a sense of what dance in preschool education is all about. In the second chapter, the content of movement is presented; these elements are the building blocks from which dance activities are created. You will want to refer frequently to this chapter when you are developing ideas into class activities. The next sections deal with preparing for dance sessions: Chapter 3 discusses general preparation, including some important ground rules; Chapter 4 takes you step by step through the process of developing an idea into a session. Chapters 5 and 6 discuss the reality of teaching a class which, as we know, never goes according to plan! Chapters 8 and 9 give suggestions for adapting material to particular groups—the very young, the handicapped, and parent-child groups. The Appendix lists ideas and resource materials; this is a section to which you will add.

Through using this book, I hope you will develop an understanding of what dance is about in the preschool setting, sense times and places in which dance can be a natural extension of your classroom activity, and develop increasing skill in planning and leading meaningful dance experiences. Finally, I hope you will feel good about making dance a regular part of the life you share with children.

Acknowledgments

The photographers—Hooshang Bagheri, Kate Barrett, Terri Detmold—who worked to capture moments of magic on film.

The teachers and children at preschools where I have worked, who helped teach *me*: Our Lady of Sorrows School (Wahiawa, Hawaii), Kawaiahao Child Care Center (Honolulu, Hawaii), Montessori Children's House (Durham, North Carolina), A Child's Garden (Greensboro, North Carolina), Guilford Technical Community College Child Care Center (Greensboro, North Carolina).

Martin Connor, Annie Dwyer, Margie Hanson, D. Michelle Irwin, and Rachel Narehood, who each made important contributions in making this book a reality.

Purposes of the American Alliance for Health, Physical Education, Recreation and Dance

The American Alliance is an educational organization, structured for the purposes of supporting, encouraging, and providing assistance to member groups and their personnel throughout the nation as they seek to initiate, develop, and conduct programs in health, leisure, and movement-related activities for the enrichment of human life.

Alliance objectives include:

1. Professional growth and development—to support, encourage, and provide guidance in the development and conduct of programs in health, leisure, and movement-related activities which are based on the needs, interests, and inherent capacities of the individual in today's society.

2. Communication—to facilitate public and professional understanding and appreciation of the importance and value of health, leisure, and movement-related activities as they contribute toward human well-being.

3. Research—to encourage and facilitate research which will enrich the depth and scope of health, leisure, and movement-related activities; and to disseminate the findings to the profession and other interested and concerned publics.

4. Standards and guidelines—to further the continuous development and evaluation of standards within the profession for personnel and programs in health, leisure, and movement-related activities.

5.   Public affairs—to coordinate and administer a planned program of professional, public, and governmental relations that will improve education in areas of health, leisure, and movement-related activities.

6.   To conduct such other activities as shall be approved by the Board of Governors and the Alliance Assembly, provided that the Alliance shall not engage in any activity which would be inconsistent with the status of an educational and charitable organization as defined in Section 501(c)(3) of the Internal Revenue Code of 1954 or any successor provision thereto, and none of the said purposes shall at any time be deemed or construed to be purposes other than the public benefit purposes and objectives consistent with such educational and charitable status.

Bylaws, Article III

CHAPTER 1

What Is Dance and Why Is It Important in Preschool?

The word *dance* brings to mind many images—ballerinas on a stage, the scene at a teenage disco, do-si-dos in a country barn, a chorus line. We see moments in sports that "look like dance," and even speak of some animal behavior as "dancing." Some people believe that dancing is always graceful and that great skill is required; some see dance as sinful self-indulgence.

Dance indeed comes in many forms, not all of them appropriate for young children. The kind of dance that is most appropriate for this age is most often referred to as *creative dance* or *creative movement.* It is an art form that is based on natural movement rather than movement of a particular style such as one might see in tap dance or ballet. But, of course, not all natural movement is *dance.* In our everyday lives we walk to a cabinet, reach up to get a box, or turn to hear someone talking, but it does not feel like dancing. Yet, a dance can be made of the same movements—walking, reaching, turning. . . . What is it that makes movement *dance*?

For a moment, try pointing to an object in the room as though you were showing someone where it is. Now, point again, but this time with a difference: Make the movement your arm performs more important than showing someone the object. This is what dance is about—making movement *itself* significant. (Otherwise, people would not bother to do it or watch it!)

How do we make movement significant? The first step is to *pay attention to it.* Most of our everyday movement is so well mastered that we no longer have any conscious awareness of what we are doing; we are "on automatic." In order to dance, we must sense ourselves just as completely as a baby taking its first tentative steps.

Perform the pointing movement again, trying to be *fully* aware. Notice if your arm moves all in one piece or if it moves sequentially (first the upper arm, then lower arm, then hand, then finger). Try it both ways and sense the difference. Does your arm feel tense or relaxed as it is pointing? Try doing it very quickly and then as though you have all the time in the world, and notice the difference. Now put your arm down and notice how it feels different from the other—you sense it more.

To dance is to discover a new world of sensory awareness. Awareness of movement is made possible by the kinesthetic sense, and it comes from the nerve endings in our joints and muscles. This sense tells us what our body is doing; it ordinarily works with the visual sense but even operates when our eyes are closed. Some degree of kinesthetic awareness is essential if we are to master skills with our bodies; the better developed it is, the more complicated the motor skills we are able to learn and perform. If the kinesthetic sense is acute, it even allows us to feel motion we see others doing; we can actually feel the tightness in a worried friend or feel a stretch in our own bodies as we watch a basketball player reach toward the basket.

Dance as we mean it here, then, refers not just to body movement, but to an inside awareness of the movement. However, dance as an art has to do not only with the body but also with the spirit, another dimension of the self. This does not mean that dance is always "expressing your feelings," but that it is more than just exercise with physical awareness. Preschool children have told me the difference between dance and other movement is that dance is *magic*. This description has been so meaningful to young children that I use it often—not in the sense of magic tricks, but in the sense of a magical state of being. Our magic comes from deep inside us, and each of us possesses it. We use our magic to transform *movement* into *dance*.

Older dancers have spoken of this "magical" power of dance using other words, such as

"Transcendence . . ."

"I lose myself . . ."

"I feel like I'm in another world . . ."

"I *am* my dance . . ."

Probably all of us have experienced transcendent moments in our lives, times of total involvement when we feel deep connection, whether it is with movement, music, or even a sunset. It is difficult to find words to talk about these experiences, because the words often do not seem to make sense in a conventional way. Philosophers who study the arts refer to such experiences as "aesthetic." While an aesthetic experience has other characteristics as well, the sense of total involvement, connection, and transformation is essential.

While we can never *make* aesthetic experiences happen, it is important to find ways to motivate or inspire children to do more than just "go through the motions" if their movement is to become the art called dance. There are a number of important considerations in helping a movement experience become more of an aesthetic experience; these will be discussed throughout this book, but particularly in the chapters on planning and teaching dance. One of these considerations is so significant that it is worth mentioning at this point: If children are to become totally involved in an experience, it must feel like it is *theirs*. Teachers can facilitate this connection—between movement and the children—by building classes around themes and ideas that have significance for these children. Even more important, the teacher must include the children's ideas whenever possible. Each child's contribution is valued, and the diversity of different ideas (different ways one can travel backwards, for example) is appreciated. The emphasis on a dance class for preschoolers is not on imitating the teacher, but on discovering the dance within each child. This is the reason it is called *creative* dance.

Preschool dance, then, is concerned with sensory awareness of movement and deep involvement in the experience. What about content? The content of dance comes primarily from movement concepts dealing with the body, space, time, energy, and relationships. (These concepts are discussed in Chapter 2.) In the preschool class, we work with these abstract concepts in concrete ways and help children see that they exist not only in dancing, but in all parts of their world. Children come to realize that they can make shapes, just as leaves and clouds have shapes; they can move with strength and lightness, just as the wind can move with these qualities. Dance becomes a way for children to know themselves and to see connections with the rest of the world.

Understanding oneself and one's relationship with the world is the most important purpose of dance (or any other art) in preschool (or any other level of education). There are, however, additional benefits that may flow from dance education in preschool. These have been recognized and valued by many teachers, although little research has been done to support these claims.

BODY AWARENESS

The development of body awareness and a clear body image (the mental picture of one's own body) can be enhanced through the preschool dance experience. This is significant for several reasons. It is important to the growth of an overall self-concept ("who I am"). The body is the first self that we know; awareness of our bodies is an important aspect of knowing ourselves. Body awareness is also an essential step in becoming aware of our feelings. Feelings do not exist just in our minds, but in our bodies as well. When we feel angry, sad, or excited, we feel it in the whole self. Getting in touch with our feelings begins with paying attention to feelings in our bodies. We then can acknowledge our feelings and deal with them in the most appropriate way.

Further, body awareness is important in the development of spatial orientation; children who do not perceive the space of their own bodies may frequently misjudge distances, bump into things, or otherwise seem not to know where they are. Body awareness also facilitates the development of motor skills: Even such seemingly simple requests as, "Don't hold your pencil so tightly" or "Move more slowly" may not mean anything to the child who is not receiving kinesthetic feedback from his or her body. Many children need appropriately structured tasks and encouragement to develop new movement skills; this feedback can lead to still greater body awareness. With greater awareness of his or her body, the child also becomes capable of greater overall self-control. Control of the body is the first kind of control children have over themselves and is the first step toward the development of internal control or "self-discipline."

CONCENTRATION AND FOCUS

Self-control is also enhanced by the capacity to concentrate and focus. In preschool dance classes, children learn what it feels like to concentrate; in fact, dance takes so much concentration that it is important that it not take the place of recess or free play. Once children learn what focusing feels like in dance, this may become a frame of reference for other activities in which concentration is more difficult to achieve. I have even had teachers of sixth graders tell me that this is the most valuable "fringe benefit" of dance. Focus and concentration are essential in creating an environment for learning in the classroom.

AWARENESS OF AND RESPECT FOR OTHERS

The learning climate in the classroom is also affected by the degree to which children are aware and respectful of each other. Experiences in dance can help children respect the working space of others, as they learn about "personal space" and "shared space." Children also learn to recognize and appreciate differences. Teachers in dance point out the different ways problems may be solved—for example, the many different ways there are to travel on a low level—and how much more interesting dance is when everyone is not doing exactly the same thing.

CONTRIBUTIONS TO CLASSROOM OPERATION

While no preschooler is always able to be self-disciplined and respectful of others, some development of these abilities facilitates smooth classroom operation. Dance can make other contributions as well to general classroom operation. Children will move anyway, and dance gives opportunities for movement that can relieve tension which will otherwise be expressed as "wiggling around." Further, children involved in dance may become more capable of discriminating what kind of movement is appropriate for different situations (when you can move freely and when you need to move more carefully, for example!)

Some of the activities suggested in this book may be used very directly as tools for improving classroom behavior. For example, teachers may tell children to "make a shape and freeze" when the classroom is too frantic, or "go out with silent, high steps" to help prevent a chaotic dash to the playground. Many of these are "tricks of the trade" for preschool teachers; they make classroom operation go more smoothly and pleasantly. There are some possible dangers in using such tricks too frequently, however, and you should guard against these. One is that we do not wish to hinder children from developing the cooperative and responsible spirit that is, in the end, the primary source of appropriate behavior. (This, of course, is a long-term goal, and we do need additional methods of encouraging acceptable behavior in the meantime!) Another danger is that children seem to be fairly canny in realizing when they are being manipulated. Many children may simply stop responding to these tricks, sensing that we have ulterior motives. It does pay to be honest with children, letting them know the need and reason to move silently or slowly or be still or get close together, and then invite them to make it fun with you. The greatest contribution to classroom behavior that dance can make comes as children gain more experience in focusing and concentrating, and develop higher levels of awareness of themselves and others.

COGNITIVE LEARNING

Cognitive learning is also stimulated by the dance experience. Movement and sensory awareness are the primary ways children learn about themselves and their world. The Swiss educator Piaget has helped us understand that children form symbols—and, therefore, language—by "internalizing movement."[1] For example, children go *up* and *down* before they know the words. Next, the words become associated with the movement and accompanying body sensations; we notice that young children cannot think or talk about movement without *doing* it. Gradually, the words begin to stand for the movements; the need to do the full movement disappears, and the movement gets smaller and smaller until we cannot see it on the outside. (It still exists inside, even though it may be reduced to only a slight degree of muscular tension.) Although we are not always aware of it, we use this internalized movement to think about things the concepts involve. Even Einstein[2] said that he made his discoveries initially

---

[1]See Furth, H.G. (1970). *Piaget for teachers* (Englewood Cliffs, NJ: Prentice Hall); or Wadsworth, B.J. (1971). *Piaget's theory of cognitive development* (New York: David McKay).

[2]See North, Marion (1973). *Movement education: Child development through motion.* New York: Dutton.

through visual and kinesthetic images of movement; he saw or *felt* an idea first and the words came later.

The important link between movement and cognitive development is a major reason why the preschool curriculum involves concrete experiences in which children may encounter and interact with their world. Words, which are abstract symbols, gain meaning only through experience with what the symbols stand for. Preschool dance provides concrete experiences in which children become more aware of movement they see in their world, try it on themselves, and notice how it feels.

Movement activities without the dance context may be used successfully as a tool for teaching a variety of concepts. Since children (as well as most adults) learn better and retain more when their whole bodies are involved, learning other subjects through movement has become both popular and valuable. As long as both the activity and subject matter are appropriate for the age group, this is a very valid way to use movement. However, when the primary goal of movement activities is to learn other subject matter, the aesthetic experience tends to get lost. Therefore, these kinds of activities are not a replacement for the kind of experience defined in this book, any more than dance is a substitute for recess or free play.

SELF-ESTEEM

As children learn more and develop new skills, their self-esteem tends to increase. Anyone who has heard a child exclaim, "I did it!" or "I know that!" recognizes the power children (as well as adults) feel in their own competence. A child's self-esteem is also enhanced through participation in activities in which his or her contributions are valued. A high level of self-esteem in turn has a positive effect on all learning: "I like myself" rapidly becomes "I can do that."

REWARDS FOR THE TEACHER

For the teacher, including dance in preschool education has many personal rewards. First, it offers a new medium for providing experiences for children. Many teachers comment that the change of pace is as stimulating to them as it is to the children. Also, dance sessions can give the sensitive teacher an opportunity to see and relate to children in a new way, to become aware of particular qualities in individual children that may ordinarily be hidden. The class clown may lose that role to reveal depth of feeling; the shy child may, even unknowingly, make an important contribution to the class. A teacher may even find enjoyment in working with a child who previously seemed hard to take.

Finally, the teacher who leads dance sessions has an opportunity to experience his or her own sense of wonder and to rediscover areas of imagination that may have long lain dormant. One classroom teacher who had begun dance with her children claimed that, because of this experience, "Wherever I look, whatever I do, I just see and feel *more* now."

More pragmatically, many preschool teachers have found that dance is very useful as an activity for parent involvement. Some preschools have included a dance performance at parent meetings and open houses. Certainly, dance is a performing art, and having a sense of performance (i.e., using full concentration, communicating with others, doing one's best, etc.) is significant in the experience. However, making a "show" for parents or other observers is almost always doomed to failure. The parents will see nothing of the magical quality the children demonstrate in the safety of their usual environment. In addition, the whole production will tend to reinforce cuteness and showing off rather than honesty of expression. There are much better ways to share this activity with parents: Either invite parents as individuals to observe your sessions, or, even better, hold a special parent-child session. (See Chapter 9.)

OTHER VALUES

There are also some reasons for including dance in preschool education that are more long range and philosophical, related to an overall perspective of education and life. If you like to think about such larger issues, you may be interested in considering these ideas too.

Many people have pondered the question, "What does it mean to be educated?" Most answers to this question include having an understanding of one's own heritage and culture and that of others. The arts, including dance, are part of the way people have responded to their world since the beginning of civilization. Of course, preschoolers are not ready to study dance history! But, just as children need to make their own stories in order to understand literature and need to paint in order to understand painting, they need to dance in order to eventually develop an understanding of this art form.

The arts have always been a way in which people have found meaning in life as well as personal exhilaration. Today, we live in a world in which people are desperately seeking meaning, "getting high," and often pursuing some dangerous ways of reaching these ends. Perhaps one of the most significant things we can teach children is how to find meaning and exhilaration in activities that will nourish them rather than destroy them. Dance is one of these activities.

Finally, dance education may have other contributions to make in helping solve complex and difficult problems that exist in our world. It is certainly unrealistic to expect that incorporating dance into preschool education might "save the world." But, surely it will help for more people to become more aware of themselves, sensitive to others, and actively conscious of the world we share.

CHAPTER 2

The Material of Movement

M*ovement* is not always *dance*. However, *dance* always involves *movement*. Movement is the raw material out of which dance is made, just as music is made from sound. The more you understand the raw material, the better you will be able to turn your ideas and those of your children into meaningful dance experiences.

If this book were a cookbook instead of a book about teaching dance, this chapter could be called "Know Your Ingredients," and I would hope that touching and tasting would be part of your experience in getting ready to cook. Similarly, I hope you will explore and experiment as you read this chapter so that you sense the movement in your body instead of just reading words.

All of the movement material discussed will be familiar to you because the examples are drawn from everyday activities. Often, though, when we stop to analyze something familiar, it begins to sound complicated. Trying out the movement for yourself will make it feel more familiar again.

I will present the movement elements in three levels, beginning with the first level of awareness experienced by the child.[1] Stop reading at the end of each level and "live with" the material for a while so it becomes meaningful as you observe children. The Teaching Ideas found in the boxes will be more useful to you as examples at this point. You may want to wait until you have read through Chapter 6 before trying them in your classroom.

LEVEL 1: THE BODY

The first level of material concerns the most obvious aspects of what the body does in movement:

- What body parts are involved.

- What action is going on.

- What body shapes are made.

This is the most important level of movement for preschool teachers to understand; it forms the emphasis of the dance activities we lead with young children.

---

[1] A number of different systems for analyzing movement have been developed by dance educators. The system developed by Rudolph Laban is probably the most widely used. See the reference by Russell (1975) in Appendix G to learn more about this system. I have drawn from Laban's work and that of others in discussing the movement elements.

Body Parts

In infants, we see that all movement makes use of the whole body; hunger, delight, and fear are expressed through total body involvement. As young children develop, we see a progression from the general to the more specific, and they gradually become capable of greater refinement, using smaller muscles and restricting movement to an isolated part or parts.

Teaching Idea: Body Parts Sing-a-Long

Concept: Body Parts

Activity: Ask children to find out if their hands can "sing" without making any noise. Play recorded music while their hands "sing along" by moving. Then, try other body parts, using small ones as well as large ones. Ask for suggestions of body parts from the children; when everyone seems to have an idea, let each child use chosen part at the same time.

Teaching Note: Use music that changes quality frequently so that all the movement will not look the same.

Experience in moving isolated body parts is important to help children develop awareness of those parts. When you observe children's drawings, you will notice that they are more aware of some parts of their bodies than others; this is true even for adults. As an experiment, close your eyes and try to sense your fingers, your lips, now your big toe, the back of your neck, your third toe; notice which parts you can feel and visualize more easily.

Body Actions

How many ways to move can you name? Walk, run, skip, hop, pull, push . . . you could probably fill a whole page with names of movements you know. Since so many movements have names, learning actions involves increasing verbal language too, particularly when children hear and/or say the name while doing the action.

Some movements make you travel across the floor, some take you up in the air, some are done while staying in one spot, and some can be done in more than one of these ways. Let's take a look at some of the most common actions.

Movements that Usually Travel Through Space

1. A *walk* is a transfer of weight from one foot to the other, with one foot always in contact with the floor.

2. A *run* is like a walk except that there is a moment when neither foot is in contact with the floor.

Teaching Note: Running is not noisy if you do it with magic and hold yourself up from the inside, instead of letting yourself be heavy on the floor. (See p. 28 of Chapter 2.)

---

3. A *leap* is like a run except that you stay in the air longer. Older children will be more successful in finding an exciting moment of suspension while they are in the air, for a sense of "flying."

4. A *gallop* is a combination of a step and a leap, in an uneven rhythm, so that the same foot is always leading. Galloping usually appears naturally by age 2½, long before skipping.

5. A *skip* is a combination of a step and a hop, in an uneven rhythm, so that the leading foot alternates. Skipping is a developmental skill that appears occasionally (rarely) by age 2½, but sometimes not until age 6 or 7. Children who have plenty of opportunities and encouragement to explore moving through space will discover a skip on their own. It is almost

never successful to teach a child to skip by practicing the step-hop. Skipping can be encouraged by taking a child's hand and skipping with him or her while chanting "one foot, other foot" in a skipping rhythm; or, while sitting, slapping the legs alternately in the skipping rhythm, using the same chant.

Movements that May or May Not Take You Through Space, but Always Take You Up in the Air

1.   A *jump* is the transfer of weight from two feet to two feet. Jumping is especially significant in that it is one of the first ways children can experience their own body weight; this facilitates development of body image.

2.   A *hop* is a transfer of weight from one foot to the same foot. This requires more balance and is, therefore, a more advanced developmental skill than jumping, just as walking appears before running. Many preschoolers cannot hop with any success before age 4.

Movements that Most Often Stay in One Place

1.   A *shake* can be a floppy wiggle or a tense vibration. (Try it out with your hand. Can you make it fast and floppy at the same time?)

2.   A *bend* and a *stretch* often go together. Bending involves closing up at body joints while stretching opens up the joints. A bend usually feels like it has a stopping point; you can bend only so far before getting "stuck" or changing into a twist. A stretch is more than just straightening; it feels like the energy keeps on going. (Sometimes, it even pulls you off balance, taking you into a run!) Try straightening and stretching your arm so you can feel the exciting difference.

3.   A *push* and a *pull* involve action similar to a bend and a stretch, but with a sense of resistance.

Teaching Note: In exploring *push* and *pull*, it is helpful for young children to first use something concrete to become aware of that feeling of resistance (i.e., push against a wall, pull one end of a rope). The emphasis should be on maintaining the force evenly rather than jerkily. Next, children can push and pull an imaginary object, trying to recall the feeling in their muscles. Finally, pushing and pulling can be performed without reference to an exterior object.

This child is pushing off to achieve elevation, and is using her arms to help get a sense of suspension. What is another suggestion you might make to her?

Teaching Note: A leap can be easier to feel if there is something to leap over and if children take a "running start" (see photo). As children are ready to increase their skills (especially around age 5), these points will help them stay in the air longer:

- Push off with the back leg and foot.
- Stretch the legs while in the air.
- Look out instead of down.
- Shoot the arms to the side, like a parachute.
- Feel light, like you really are suspended in the air.

4.   A *twist* and a *turn* both involve rotation, but there is an important difference. To experience twisting, rotate your neck to the right as far as it will go, and then to the left. One end is fixed, so there is a limit to how

much the other end can move. Twisting is not possible at all joints of the body without injury; you should be sensitive when asking children to twist body parts.

In turning, both ends are free to move all the way around; individual body parts thus cannot turn. Other words for turning include *spinning, whirling,* and *twirling.* Cartwheels, somersaults, and rolling are special kinds of turns.

5.   A *rise* and *sink* are often performed sequentially. They allow us to change levels between low and high.

6.   Both a *balance* and a *fall* provide excitement in dance. The balance is the moment of suspension created as all body parts stretch away from the body center. You can experience this suspension while sitting in a chair: Shift your weight to one hip, and now stretch at all of your joints (including the hip) to balance. Notice how this feels different from just sitting on one hip: The stretch is what is holding you up.

A fall is created when the body weight goes beyond the point of balance.

Teaching Note: While children are much less likely than adults to injure themselves while falling, they should understand some basic principles of safety. One is to fall on body parts that are soft (buttocks) rather than hard (heads) or pointed (elbows, knees). Another is to lower the weight gradually, rolling it down to take the weight sequentially from one part to another, rather than letting it all hit the floor at once. Children can find ways to fall without getting hurt and can understand the difference between falling in a dance and falling so it hurts. ("In a dance," one child said, "it feels like you're pulling yourself down.").

---

7.   A *swing* and a *sway* are similar in many ways. Swinging is a very exhilarating, freeing movement that sounds "technical" as we describe it: A fall, giving into gravity, followed by a rebound to a suspension point before the fall begins again. Swinging requires some risk and daring, but it is the daring that makes it exhilarating; it cannot be done halfway. If you "hold back" in doing a swing, it becomes a sway—a more controlled, even shifting of weight. Experiment until you can find the difference between these two movements; this will help you identify them as you observe them in children.

There are many other action words and many ways to move that do not have names. Often, these are variations of the basic actions listed above, but we can help children to expand their movement and verbal vocabularies by using descriptive words. Some of these are:

Crumple, settle, and melt

Explode and burst

Gather and scatter

Curl and uncurl

Slither

Zoom

Flicker, skitter, and scamper

Tiptoe

Inch

Make a list of other movement words you can think of.

Even while every child in the class is responding to the same action word, they may very well be doing something different. Try out, for example, how many ways you can find to walk or to shake. We can make a movement different by using different body parts (Can your fingers walk? Can your toes shake?) and by changing something about the space, timing, or energy. (More about that in Level II.)

Teaching Idea: Magic Soup

Concept: Movement Words

Activity: Use any container as an imaginary soup pot. (A single-head drum works well, but so does a small trash can.) Ask children for suggestions of what would go into magic soup, and make a ceremony of mixing it. Then taste it and find that it has become running soup; everyone who tastes it begins to run. Give all the children a taste, so all can run. Give the signal to freeze, and then discover it has become tiptoe soup. Repeat with any other movement words.

Teaching Note: Be sure to alternate vigorous movement with less vigorous movement. (It could even be resting soup!) Also, Level II concepts in movement can be used, such as slow motion, backwards, etc.

Body Shape

Our bodies make many shapes during a day's work, but we tend to be even less aware of these shapes than we are of our actions. Similarly, children tend to become aware of movement before they become aware of shape. For a moment, become aware of your body's position as you sit in your chair. Now, instead of letting the chair hold you up, *hold yourself up* from the inside, so you are aware of the space you fill up. This is what makes a shape in dance; it is different from just a position. Try to sense your shape from the inside as well as visualizing it. Shift to another shape, being aware both as you move and as you are still. This kind of perception of the body is a new and exciting discovery for preschoolers.

The first step in a preschooler's discovery of shape is learning to *freeze.* To freeze movement is more than just stopping it; it is a sense of actively "holding on" to keep the movement from happening and it has a sense of readiness to begin again.

Making a shape is different from lying on the floor.

Teaching Idea: Shake and Freeze

Concepts: Shaking Body Parts; Freezing

Activity: Shake arms very hard and fast; freeze suddenly when teacher gives the signal. Notice how the arms tingle inside. Repeat with other body parts and the whole self.

Teaching Note: Point out to the children the magical, exciting feeling in the air when everyone is frozen.

Moving from the freeze to the concept of shape is fairly simple. One very successful way is to do different move and freeze activities and notice the different shapes in which children freeze. Point out these differences. Then, see if the children can maintain their shapes while you pick them up and move them to another spot; they must hold themselves up from the inside if they are to keep a shape! (Preschool children are light enough to lift if they are holding up their own weight. For a further discussion of weight, see page 28 of Chapter 2.)

This one is really a shape; it doesn't fall apart when I pick it up.

Sometimes, you may use specific shapes (of leaves, flowers, clouds, letters) as a stimulus for exploration. Such words usually lead to very limited shape exploration. Instead of asking children to "make a leaf shape," it usually works better to ask them to explore more general shape words that describe leaves. For example, you might say, "Some leaves have points; can you make a shape with points?" Some other examples of general shape words are:

Curved

Angular (pointed)

Straight

Wide/narrow

Flat/curled

Large/small

Twisted

With holes

(Holes? We are talking about what dancers call *negative space*—space around or inside a shape, made when body parts enclose or partially enclose space.)

Teaching Idea: A Magician Makes Shapes

Concept: Shapes

Activity: Chant or sing this direction for the children, while they follow it:
Turn around, turn around,
Turn around, turn around,
Turn around, make a new shape,
And *freeze* it.

Teaching Note: (1) The sense of magic in your voice helps bring about a magical quality in children's movement. (2) Acknowledge something special about each child's shape at some point during the activity.

Shapes are not always frozen; we also make shapes as we move. Shaping refers to changing from one shape to another to another, constantly maintaining an awareness of shape. (For a favorite activity involving shaping, see the story of The Ship-Shape Shape Shop in Appendix D.)

Shaping: Changing your shape while traveling.

LEVEL II: SPACE, ENERGY, AND TIME

The second level of awareness of movement involves factors that modify basic action, either where we do it, the amount or kind of energy we use, or our use of time. Most of these factors can be explored by preschool children, even though all of them have subtleties with which even advanced dancers work.

Remember as you read this section that these factors are abstract concepts that preschoolers do not understand. Only the movement is meaningful to them. (The analysis I have provided is for *you*!) It is from these movement experiences, however, that abstract concepts eventually form.

Space Factors

The space factors describe differences in where we go as we move. They give us many possibilities for changing the basic movement of Level I. The space factors you will want to explore with preschoolers are:

- Direction—Forward, backwards, sideways, up, down.

- Size—Large and small movements.

- Pathway—Patterns we make as we move through the air or on the floor.

- Level—Primarily high and low. More advanced children can also explore middle level.

- Focus—Where the eyes look.

Direction

Directions can be considered in two ways—according to the body or according to the room. A teacher should understand both in order to avoid confusing children.

In terms of the body:

Forward is where your nose leads you.

Backwards is where your back leads you.

Sideways is where the side of your body leads you.

Up is where the top of your head leads you.

Down is where the bottom of your feet go.

In terms of the room:

Forward is toward the designated front of the room
    (even if you are walking "backwards").

Backwards is toward the back of the room.

Sideways is toward the side of the room
    (toward the piano or the aquarium or . . .).

Up is toward the ceiling.

Down is toward the floor.

Be sure the children understand which "forward" you mean when you work with directions!

Working with directions lends itself very easily to images. What things can you think of that change direction—a robot, a helicopter, drifting smoke?

Teaching Idea: New Crab Walks

Concept: Direction, Traveling Movement

Activity: Observe and/or describe a crab's movement: Tiny steps that go forward, backwards, sideways. Explore making tiny steps while going forward, then backwards, then sideways, changing on cue. When the children clearly understand the difference, ask them to find other ways to travel in each direction.

Teaching Note: At first, tell the children when to change direction and which direction to use. Then, ask the children to be their "own teacher"—to tell themselves which direction when you just say "change." Some children may even be able to tell themselves *when* to change.

Size

Exploring the size of movement is important for preschoolers. It helps them learn the meaning of big and small as well as the limits of their own bodies. Most movements can be varied by changing the size—a large wiggle or a small one, a big jump or a little one. Doing large movements comes naturally to most preschoolers and helps them "let off steam." Making a movement small takes more concentration and often results in a very magical quality. ("Make a shake so small that no one else can see it.")

Teaching Idea: Big Steps, Small Steps

Concept: Size

Activity: Play a big (loud) sound on a drum and then a small (quiet) sound. Ask the children to take big steps when they hear the big sound and small steps when they hear the small sound. (Use other kinds of movement besides walking, too).

Teaching Note: (1) Give the children a moment for stillness in between the changes so they can be "ready." (Otherwise, this is likely to be a game accompanied by shrieks and shouts!) (2) Older children can also identify an in-between (medium-sized) sound and movement.

Level

Level refers to vertical distance from the floor—whether one is low, high, or in the middle. In dance, levels are usually described in relation to an individual's body, so that high level for an adult is much higher than high level for a child. For small children, middle level is harder to find because there is not much space in between high and low.

Level may describe shape (making a high shape, a low shape, a middle-level shape) or movement (as in low rolling or slithering, high tip-toeing or jumping).

Teaching Idea: Magic Forest

Concepts: Level, Shape

Activity: Following a walk through the woods, discuss things that are high in the forest (trees, vines, birds) and things that are low (mushrooms, fallen branches). Notice their different shapes. Explore growing into different high shapes and different low shapes. Create a story about a magic dancing forest in which things grow and change into new high shapes and low shapes.

Teaching Note: If the growing always happens slowly, children will lose interest quickly. Also explore growing quickly, "popping" into the new level.

Focus

For preschool children, work with focus is limited to visual focus—where you are looking while moving or still. Focus may be fixed directly on one spot or may be a roving focus (looking all around). Direct focus is usually introduced as part of *freezing,* telling children to "freeze your whole self, even your eyes."

Pathways

Pathways are designs the body makes in space. Drawing and writing involve making pathways on paper; in dance, we make pathways in the air and on the floor. To make a circular pathway in the air, draw a circle in the air with one finger, with an elbow, and with your big toe. If you run in a circle, you are making a circular pathway on the floor.

Movement activities involving pathways help children develop skills used in writing and copying and even map reading!

Teaching Idea: Dance of the Small Animals (from a Native American theme)

Concept: Small Steps, Focus

Activity:

1. Brief discussion: Native Americans sometimes danced about the animals they knew. Small animals take small steps and always must be on the lookout for danger.

2. Take small steps traveling across the floor. As you move, let your eyes look all around. When you hear a loud (drum) sound, *freeze* and freeze your eyes looking where the sound came from.

Teaching Note: Give the freeze signal from a different place in the room each time.

Teaching Idea: Magic Paint

Concept: Pathway

Activity: Dip specified body parts into "magic paint" and fill the air and/or floor with curves, zig-zags, spots, or . . . Be sure to make large ones and small ones, up high and down low. Make the last one in a very small place.

Teaching Note: Music or singing as accompaniment will be very important to keep this activity going.

Energy Factors

This aspect of movement is concerned with the amount of energy used and how it is released. Unlike the factors we have discussed up to now, energy itself is not visible. It is experienced internally, and only its results may be observed. A study of energy in movement can very easily become complex and abstract. Yet, more than any other aspect, it is the source of movement itself. There are a number of ways of thinking about and categorizing energy qualities. Three particular concepts of energy are especially important in preschool dance and are appropriate for preschoolers to explore. These are:

*   Tension/relaxation

- Flow: bound/free

- Weight: strong/light

These categories are not totally separate but have a definite relationship with each other.

Tension/Relaxation

When you are moving, you can stop yourself by using either tension or relaxation. Tension feels hard and tight; relaxation feels soft, loose, and floppy. If we are either completely tense or completely relaxed, we cannot move.

Very often, children who seem frequently out of control do not know how to slow or stop themselves except by using tension. Tightness is very useful for stopping yourself suddenly. However, when we try to use tension to hold ourselves back for very long, the tension increases more and more until we explode. This is why it is important for children to learn how to make their bodies relax.

Some children—and many adults—have great difficulty using relaxation. Practice in using total relaxation is a valuable part of a dance session.

Teaching Note: I have found it especially helpful to suggest that relaxation happens on the inside; it feels like you are soft and melted inside.

Teaching Idea: Tight and Loose

Concepts: Tension and Relaxation; Body Parts

Activity: Show the children two contrasting objects, one that feels hard and tight and one that is soft and loose (for example, a hard plastic doll and a rag doll or a highly inflated basketball and a deflated ball). Give children an opportunity to touch each and feel the difference.

While the children lie on the floor, call out the names of individual body parts and ask the children to make them hard and tight, then soft and melted. Check them to be sure that they are really releasing in the relaxation. If a child is having difficulty, give him or her a chance to "check" your muscles to feel the difference.

Teaching Note: Make sure that your voice reflects the qualities you are asking the children to use, as they will be responding as much to your voice as to your words.

Most activities dealing purely with tension and relaxation, such as the one described here, have more to do with stillness and stopping than with moving. When we think about various degrees of tension and relaxation in movement, we are really thinking about *flow*.

Flow: Bound or Free

The factor of *flow* is apparent in an infant's earliest movement. Flow has to do with the "ongoingness" of movement. When we release energy freely, pulling out all the stops, we describe the movement as *free flow*. When you move with free flow, it is hard to stop yourself right away. Try doing large body swings or fast running to see if you can reach a level of free flow.

Bound *flow* refers to releasing our energy in a controlled, restrained manner so that we are readily able to stop ourselves. The movement feels more careful—perhaps even cautious. Try moving in the same pathway as if you were swinging, but hold onto your weight rather than releasing it into gravity; when you use bound flow, the movement stops being a swing. Bound flow uses more tension than free flow.

Most young children use free flow movement very readily as they grow and experience themselves and their world. (If a young child always uses bound flow, it could indicate some underlying problem; you should explore the reason the child always "holds back".[2] Children need many opportunities to move safely with free flow—to run freely, to jump and fall, to fingerpaint on large pieces of paper. If we do not provide opportunities for children to move with free flow, they will usually make their own opportunities.

Teaching Note: In teaching a dance class, you need to watch the children for signals that they are ready to change from bound to free flow, to provide contrasting experience. You will see a bursting out of energy and/or an inability to maintain concentration if you stay with highly controlled movement for too long.

It is also important, however, that children be able to use bound flow at appropriate times—to be able to move through the classroom with care for others, to be able to keep paint on the paper when necessary. Some children have more difficulty than others in controlling their movement. (When children are always out of control, we also suspect some sort

---

[2]For a discussion of the relationship between personality and movement, see Marion North, *Personality Assessment Through Movement*. London: Macdonald & Evans, 1972.

of a problem; such children are very challenging for teachers as well as parents.)

A great many children have trouble stopping themselves at one time or another. Awareness of the tension/relaxation factor can help them develop this skill.

Weight: Strength and Lightness

When most people think of weight, they think of heaviness. In dance, heavy movement is very relaxed; it is also referred to as *passive weight*. Try moving with passive weight: Stay as relaxed and heavy as possible, but use just enough energy to get yourself moving into a walk. This is the way most people walk a good bit of the time. If you try dancing in this heavy, passive state, it probably will not feel much like dancing.

Dancing with heaviness, then, is more about relaxation than weight. The category of *weight* in dance is about actively supporting your own weight. To find this active use of weight, try the following: Make a shape, but instead of using complete tension, stay just hard enough to hold up your shape. (It feels something like egg whites when they are beaten until stiff enough to hold a peak!) Try to keep this same degree of tension/relaxation while you do a normal walk; you are now actively holding up your own weight but have the freedom to move.

Once you are actively holding up your own weight, you can use it—to move with strength (force) or lightness. Try walking through space like you are "pushing your weight around." Feel strong and forceful, but not overly tight or tense. When we see people move with forcefulness, we sense that they are assertive and know what they are doing. We use strength not only to knead dough and push furniture, but to take charge of an overly noisy classroom.

In looking at the active use of weight, the opposite of strong is not weak (which is *heavy*), but light. Try walking with a gentle, delicate step so you feel nearly weightless. We often use lightness in the classroom when dealing with shy children or when trying to avoid disturbing a child's concentration.

Adults are much more skillful than children at using the extremes of strength and lightness. Children may tighten their muscles excessively in order to achieve strength or lightness. When this happens, they are using *bound flow* instead of *weight*.

Teaching Note: If children are using tension instead of strength, suggest that they try being strong and tight, then strong and *not* tight. (A big bear is strong, but not tight!) This will still be difficult for preschoolers to accomplish!

Teaching Idea: Make It Strong, Make It Light

Concept: Strength and Lightness; Basic Actions

Activity: Select different action words; perform each one with strength and then lightness.

> *Walk:* Walk as though making deep footprints in the sand; next, walk so lightly you would not leave footprints.

> *Run:* Run with strength, pushing the air out of the way as you go; next, run with lightness so you make hardly any wind as you go by.

> *Touch:* Touch the floor with enough strength to squash a bug; now touch it as though it were a dandelion puff that you must not destroy.

Find other images to use with other action words and ask the children for their suggestions.

Teaching Note: Make sure that your accompaniment and your voice reflect the quality you are trying for. It is very difficult to move lightly to a loud voice and pounding drum!

Time Factors

Timing has to do with the relationship of one movement or part of a movement to another. Children must first develop an awareness of time within their bodies before they can sense it in music or deal with it as an abstraction. The time factors we deal with in preschool dance are:

- Pulse
- Speed
- Duration
- Rhythm
- Phrasing

Pulse
Most music that we hear has a metric rhythm in which sounds are divided into equal beats. The *pulse* of music refers to the ongoing underlying beat. The effect of a strong pulse is very powerful. It is practically impossible to listen to a Sousa march or rock music without feeling an internal re-

sponse. When the internal response becomes external, as it does very readily, movement results: We tap our foot, clap hands, or join in and move along. There is a great deal of satisfaction in this kind of movement, as it makes us feel part of a group. This is one reason why social, folk, and square dances are so enjoyable.

Not all dance movement or dance is based on metric rhythm. Other kinds of movement involve *organic rhythm*—breathing, an ocean wave building and crashing, the wind blowing a tree, a butterfly emerging from a chrysalis, a bird soaring. Preschool dance should also include this kind of movement, which "unfolds in its own time."

Being able to "stay on the beat" is a necessary skill for many music activities. Because a strong beat is so powerful, most preschool children can move with a beat as long as

- The beat is not too fast or too slow.

- You do not make the child overanxious about the task.

If a child is having trouble staying with a beat, it is usually better to change the beat rather than to exhort the child to listen more carefully. The child needs to experience *being* with the beat, internalizing it, before *adapting* to it.

Teaching Note: The dullest ways to work on staying with the beat are clapping and walking to a drum sound. Other basic actions are much more interesting; also, using a variety of sounds for accompaniment, including music with a strong beat, will maintain interest. You can begin by providing an appropriate pulse for basic actions such as jumping and tiptoeing. Then, you can ask, "Does this sound make you feel like jumping or tiptoeing?" and give children an opportunity to move to the beat.

Speed

The *speed* (or *tempo*) of movement refers to how fast or slow it is. These are, of course, relative terms. What initially seems slow may look fast when compared to something even slower. This level of understanding (the "relativeness" of speed) requires an ability to form concepts. The goal of working with speed in preschool is to know what "fast" and "slow" feel like inside.

Teaching Idea: Swallow the Bounce

Concept: Pulse

Activity: Play music with a strong beat. Tell the children that there is a bounce in that music and that if they "swallow" it, it will make them bounce, too. (You may wish to make a "ceremony" when each child picks the bounce out of the air and swallows it.) Then discover what the beat makes them do besides bounce: jog, jump, etc. Also try putting the bounce in a single body part and making the bounce smaller or larger.

Teaching Note: Acknowledge the individual responses children make so they will understand there is no one right way to respond to a pulse.

Because children have smaller bodies than adults, the same movement usually does not take as long; for this reason, children often interpret speed differently than adults. "Slow" for a child may well be faster than it is for an adult. (How many times have you told a young child to "slow down"?)

In addition to the difficulty of interpretation, many children have difficulty accomplishing slow movement. As previously discussed, they may not know how to slow down except by using excess tension, and they can maintain this tension for only so long before bursting out again. Success in using relaxation usually precedes real mastery of slow motion.

Despite these obstacles, work with fast and slow movement is very valuable for preschoolers. Slow motion tends to have a magical quality about it and, many times, a child's first experience of the magical quality of dance comes during slow motion.

Teaching Idea: Slow Feet, Fast Feet

Concepts: Speed, Traveling Movement

Activity: What if your feet were magic and changed from slow feet to fast feet whenever they wanted? Suggest various traveling movements for children to try with slow feet and then fast feet, changing back and forth several times. Ask the children to suggest what kind of traveling movements to use.

Teaching Note: Begin by giving the children a signal for when to change from slow to fast. After they can do this, you may wish to try giving them an opportunity to decide when to change from slow to fast.

Duration

Duration means the length of time movement lasts—a long time, a short time, or something in between. It is often but not always related to speed. (You can move fast for a long time or slowly for a short time.) This concept is preparatory for an understanding of note values in music, but we do not introduce it in this context.

> *Teaching Note:* When exploring the basic actions with children, include variations in duration: shake your hands for a long time, shake your head for a short time, etc.

Rhythm Patterns

Patterns are made by arranging long and short sounds or strong and light sounds. Say your own name out loud; clap the pattern and then let your feet stamp it. Most preschoolers do not have the auditory discrimination or body control to accurately follow complicated rhythm patterns.

> *Teaching Idea:* Echo
>
> *Concept:* Rhythm Pattern
>
> *Activity:* Clap a simple rhythm such as galloping:____ __ ____ __ ____ __ ____ . Ask the children to clap it immediately afterwards, as an echo. Repeat several times and then ask if they can *gallop* as the echo. Try the same thing with a different rhythm, such as strong, even beats for jumping. Then ask the children if they can listen to the sound you make and find the movement echo that fits.
>
> *Teaching Note:* This kind of activity can very easily become a competitive game focused on getting the right answer. Try very hard to avoid this emphasis. Remember, a child may hear something different in your clap and you need to give children the opportunity to find their own answers. At the preschool level, we are more concerned with becoming aware of rhythm patterns than with accurately reproducing them.

Phrases

Phrases are longer sequences of movement that have a sense of completion by themselves. We may think of a phrase as a "dance sentence." You can make a phrase by putting different action words together rhythmically. Some examples are

> Gallop & gallop & gallop & gallop & twirl around and freeze.
>
> Curl up very slowly—uncurl very fast!

LEVEL III: RELATIONSHIP

The third level of movement awareness has to do with the relationships created through movement—relationships between body parts, different movements and shapes, individuals, and groups, as well as with the environment. Some of the concepts of relationship are:

- Toward and away from
- Around
- Through
- Between
- Over and under
- Before and after
- Faster and slower
- Alike and different

These are concepts children build during their preschool years through their movement experiences.

Preschool children tend to see the world from their own point of view; so, their success in working with a partner or group is correspondingly limited. Therefore, the kinds of relationships primarily dealt with in preschool dance are those between body parts, between different movements and shapes, and between the individual child and some aspect of the environment.

Relationship of Body Parts

Explore for a moment what your hands can do with each other. They can come together and go apart, one hand can be on top of the other, or one hand can make a tunnel for a finger to go through. You can make both hands look the same and then different. You can also let hands relate to other parts—shake a hand over your head or behind your shoulder or next to your knee; let one hand connect to different body parts.

> *Teaching Note:* Whenever you are exploring body parts or basic actions of a part, include aspects of relationship among possibilities to explore.

Relationships Between the Child and the Environment

You help a child become more aware of his or her environment by relating to it. Can you find a negative space (hole) in the room that is large enough for your whole body to fit in? (Under a table?) Can you find small ones just the right size for your finger to fit? What in the room could you go all the way around, or into, or over? Can you find a corner (angular shape) in a body part and connect it to a corner in the room? Such questions require us to expand our senses beyond our immediate selves and connect to the environment we occupy.

> *Teaching Idea:* Moonbeam (or Sunbeam)
>
> *Concept:* Relating to the Environment; Lightness; Focus
>
> *Activity:* Show the children a picture or photograph in which light is reflected off different objects. (Pictures of water are especially useful.) It looks like the moonlight (or sunlight) is touching the objects, making them magical. Ask the children if they can touch a part of themselves as lightly as a moonbeam; let them try running as softly as moonlight. Then ask them what they would like to touch if they were a moonbeam; see if they can first find it with their eyes, and then travel lightly there to touch it with moonlight. Repeat, having them find the object with their eyes each time before they begin to travel. Ask them to find new places they hadn't noticed before.
>
> *Teaching Note:* It may be difficult for children to maintain the magical lightness for long; be ready to change to another activity before it is lost. Light, magical accompaniment will add to the quality of this activity.

Props can also be introduced to become part of the environment. The list of props that can be used is practically endless. There are two general ways of working with a prop in dance, but they are often connected in the same lesson.

One way to work with a prop is to hold it or otherwise attach it to the body and dance *with* it. Some common examples are scarves, crepe paper streamers, paper plates, sheets of plastic wrap, small hand instruments, balloons, capes, and ribbons (which can be tied to different body parts). The children explore to see what they can make the prop do. You may stimulate exploration with such cues as, "Can you take it high and low? Can you make circles with it? Can you shake it?"

Another way to work with a prop is to put it on the floor and find ways to relate to it. All of the props listed can be used in this way as well as cardboard boxes, chairs, carpet squares, hula hoops, pillows—even grocery bags and plastic bowls. You may stimulate exploration with such cues as, "Can you jump over it? Can you gallop around it? Can you put one part of you inside it?"

Props introduce an exciting element into a dance class, but they may also introduce a problematic one. As with other potential problems, some advance planning can be helpful. For example, young children usually need a chance to *mess* with a prop before they can begin to *work* with it. You may even wish to introduce the prop on an earlier day for this purpose. The only difficulty then may be making the transition between playtime and dance time. An adult's temptation is usually to make this transition too soon. When it is time to make the shift, you need to make this very clear to the children. It will also help to have the children put the prop on the floor—so they are not touching it at all—to listen for directions, and to begin with very structured, teacher-directed manipulation of the prop (which may be based on the movement you observed as the children were playing).

Teaching Idea: Hat Dance

Concept: Relating to a Prop

Activity: Give each child a hat. Give several suggestions regarding ways to relate: jump over it, tiptoe around it, push it, wear it on a part of your body besides your head, use it as a drinking cup (or a pillow or a kitten or . . .) Ask the children for their suggestions. All of these things can be part of the dance they do with their hat . . . everything except wearing it on their head! (You may also wish to rule out throwing it up and catching it, as children can easily get stuck with this and lose a sense of dance!) Play music for the Hat Dance. Give them a signal to indicate "Change and do something else with your hat."

Teaching Note: During the dance, use your voice to acknowledge each child's ideas or to suggest ideas to a child who seems "lost."

Never, even in the playtime with the prop, allow the children to be destructive. They should become accustomed to treating all props with care, even inexpensive and sturdy ones, or they will never be able to make the transition to the special quality needed for dance. Remove the prop if it is not treated with care.

Relationships Between Movements and Shapes

To see different movements and shapes in relationship to each other is the first step leading to dance composition, in which we make choices to make dance look more interesting: a slow movement followed by a quick one, making a high shape and a low one instead of making both the same level. Obviously, dance composition is not a goal for preschoolers. However, they are ready to notice obvious relationships between movements, just as they notice that the wind blows strong and then gently, or that one gerbil is going faster than the others.

Teaching Note: During dance sessions (as well as other times), you can help children expand their awareness by pointing out "accidental" relationships. "Look, John has a high shape next to Chris' low one." You can also set up problems of relationship within the context of other explorations: "If I walk fast, can you walk faster?" "Let's make a dance with three parts—two the same and one different (e.g., tiptoe . . . tiptoe . . . roll)."

Teaching Idea: Surprise Dance

Concept: Contrasting Relationships Between Movements

Activity: Begin with a basic traveling action, such as walking or galloping, for everyone to do together. Play a steady beat for accompaniment or use music. Then, give a signal for the children to stop and do a different movement—and to make it a surprise. Then resume the traveling action and repeat.

Teaching Note: Help the children notice what is different through such comments as, "Matthew's is different because he isn't using his feet. Karen's is different because it's very slow."

Stretch until it pulls you into a fall.

REVIEW

Level I: The Body
    A. Body parts
    B. Basic actions
    C. Body shapes

Level II: Space, Energy, and Timing
    A. Space factors
       1. Direction
       2. Size
       3. Level
       4. Focus
       5. Pathways
    B. Energy factors
       1. Tension/relaxation
       2. Flow: bound/free
       3. Weight: strength/lightness

    C. Timing factors
      1. Pulse
      2. Speed
      3. Duration
      4. Rhythm
      5. Phrasing

Level III: Relationship
    A. Relationships between body parts
    B. Relationships with the environment and props
    C. Relationships between movements and shapes

Although we have discussed them as separate elements, all levels of movement exist at the same time. Sometimes, one aspect of a movement may seem most important—perhaps its speed—but, if we look again, we see that it is also a forward run, using the feet, making a vertical shape, etc. Young children do not see these aspects of movement simultaneously so it is very appropriate to deal with them one at a time.

Hopefully, you now have a greater understanding of the *stuff* of which dance is made; now we are ready to discuss doing it with children.

CHAPTER 3

Preparing for Dance

Many of the best moments in teaching come without any prior planning. Some sessions grow out of the magic of a moment shared with even one or two children. Perhaps a child notices a leaf fall floating to the ground and says, "I can do that," or, in the middle of hearing a story, a child makes the action of the words come alive. The dance may then be finished, or perhaps others may spontaneously come and join, and you feel the closeness of an inspired time that you never could have planned for. Sometimes you, as the teacher, may even initiate such moments, stimulated by an unexpected happening, but you may very well end up feeling unnecessary.

This indeed is the way children naturally experience their world, using all of their senses, and their bodies as well as their minds, so that *learning* is the same as *being*. Hopefully, as you become more attuned to movement and dance, more of these moments will occur in your classroom—and out of it. At such times, questions of whether or not you have the right space, length of time, or number of children are irrelevant.

However, there will be times when you will want to plan a session for more depth, just as you appreciate the unexpected discoveries that lead to spontaneous science experiences, but still feel the need to set up situations that can allow for more in-depth experimenting. These are the times when you will wish to garner all your resources, and try to structure a situation that will foster in-depth understanding, yet be as magical as the spontaneous ones. Let's look at some preparations that can help make these sessions work better.

OVERALL CONSIDERATIONS: SPACE, SCHEDULES, NUMBERS, DRESS

Before you ever begin to think about leading a specific session, there are certain items you will need to consider. One of the most obvious is *SPACE*. First of all, you will look at the *size* of your space: How large is it? How many children can move comfortably in their own place and how many can move through space? The shape is important too; a long and narrow room will not serve as many children as a square one because you need to be able to see each child. If your space seems too small for your whole group to move freely, consider:

- Moving the furniture all the way back into the corners and putting chairs on top of tables.

- Using some furniture as natural obstacles (going over, under, around, etc.).

- Dividing your children into smaller groups, perhaps trading off with another teacher at some point during the day.

- Doing *some* kinds of movement activities with the whole class, saving running through space and similar activities for outdoors or when part of the class is involved elsewhere.

A space can also be too large. A very large open space, such as a gymnasium, may simply invite children to run to the distant corners. This is fine for recess/free play, but not for an activity needing close concentration. Also, all children should be able to hear you when you speak in a normal voice . . . and hopefully also in a magic whisper. If the room is too large, find something to use to define the boundaries of your dancing space.

The *floor* in your space should be smooth and warm enough for children to move safely in bare feet. (Also see the discussion under *DRESS*.) Other *safety* factors may need consideration, too. There should be no sharp points or items that might be disastrous if run into (the aquarium, for instance). Also, beware of a wet floor near the water table!

Think about what *distractions* are present or likely to be present in your space. This category may include stored items that may be too tempting for the children to resist exploring. You probably do not want to spend your energy and dance time saying, "Stay away from that," over and over. Can you remove the items or make them look uninteresting? (For example, cover them or turn them around to face the wall.) It is also helpful to have children put away toys and materials; have clean up time before dance begins. Interruptions are also likely to be very distracting in any activity working for high concentration. If people always seem to be going in and out of your space, you may want to consider a polite sign on your door.

Also consider the *aesthetics* of the space. Does it invite a magical quality? You may not be able to do anything about peeling paint, but it is possible to empty an overflowing trash can and straighten a picture on the wall.

Is it all right to work *outdoors*? Some kinds of activities will work outside but, in most cases, it is not an ideal space for dance. It frequently is too large, has a surface that demands footwear, and is filled with distractions. It usually takes much more work to get the quality you are seeking, especially when children are just beginning to understand this quality.

But, what if you do not have a perfect space? You will rarely have the ideal space in which to work! You have to adjust, adapt, or eliminate some kinds of activities (and perhaps discover others) because of the limitations.

You must also consider when to *SCHEDULE* the sessions. The best time of day is always when it feels right, when children are ready to enter into the magic with you. You probably already plan your schedule to alternate between group and individual activities, between quiet and vigorous ones. Even though dance is a very personal experience, it is also a *group* activity. Dance works best when children are ready to come together, not when they have had their full of the group and need to work alone. I remember one "failure" of a session that I was unable to figure out until the teacher told me the schedule had changed that morning and the children had spent an unusually long period listening and singing together just before I arrived. The children were ready for free play, and they let me know!

It is important to remember that *dance is not a substitute for recess or free play.* It requires a great deal of concentration. But, children also need time to "mess around" and to play on their own, even on days when the weather prohibits outdoor play. Many of the activities suggested in this book could also be done as games or other free or organized play, but it is important that you recognize, and for the children to recognize, that dance is a *special* way of moving.

If you wish to schedule a session right after playground time, you must ordinarily plan on an extra amount of time for transition if the children are to have the kind of concentration you desire. (See the discussion of transitions in Chapter 4.)

How much *time* should you allow for a session? It is the children who determine the length of every session, whether it be spontaneous or planned, in the sense that, when *they* are finished, there is no way to make *dance* continue. (They may continue to go through the motions, but it will not be *dance* anymore.) You will find that the sessions will tend to be fairly short at first, but will lengthen as the year goes along, up to 30 or 40 minutes in a typical classroom. For planned sessions, you will gradually learn about how long you can expect the children to "stay with" you (although they will sometimes surprise you). Flexibility is necessary in dealing with time. You must know what to suggest as the next activity if the session ends earlier than you expect. It is also frustrating to have to bring a session to a close when you are in the middle of something wonderful just because it is time for another scheduled activity.

In considering the *NUMBER* of children you can accommodate, you will need to think first of all of the space you have. Your own confidence and experience are also determining factors. At the beginning, especially if you are an inexperienced teacher, you should feel free to start with just a few children. (If all the children in your classroom are not participating, however, you will need to plan what to do with the others so that they are not disturbing.) As you gain more experience, you can expect to be able to handle larger numbers. The structure of the class will change as the numbers increase. (See Chapter 4 on planning the individual session.)

With assistance, you can expect to handle even more children. If you have the luxury, having another teacher handle problems (tying of hair ribbons, the bumped knee, toileting accidents) is wonderful; it is essential with groups larger than about 15.

Ordinarily, ages and social grouping of children also affect the numbers you can handle. Your preschool may be organized so that age groups are separate, or with a span of ages represented in each class. However the age groups are organized, it is most helpful to keep the children in groups to which they are accustomed. It will be more difficult if you also have to develop a sense of "being a group" with children who come from different classrooms and are not accustomed to interacting with each other.

Many teachers prefer to teach mixed-age groups, as the younger children do learn so much from the older ones. The sessions proposed in this book are planned for this type of grouping. A group of all younger children ("younger" refers as much to maturity as it does to age!) will need simpler, shorter activities; you may need to adapt the classes if you teach only 3-year-olds. Similarly, you will be able to do more complex activities if you have only 5-year-olds in your group.

The *DRESS* for creative dance ordinarily makes no difficult demands on children or teachers. Children should be dressed so that they can move comfortably and safely. Since most preschoolers wear play clothes, the only real "issue" here tends to be shoes and socks. The appropriate attire for this activity is bare feet, so that the children can have maximum control of their movement and have this important body part free. Many adults dislike going barefoot. Try not to transmit your own preference for wearing footwear to the children. Shoes are not only restrictive but a potential source of danger; in dance sessions, toes can get stepped on and even heads can get accidentally kicked if a child is making an upside-down shape. On most surfaces, wearing only socks or tights is also dangerous, inviting sliding and falling. It is highly unlikely that going barefoot on a carpeted surface for a half hour will be detrimental to anyone's health. If you must work on a cold, bare tile floor in the winter, however, it may be necessary for the children to keep their feet covered; the activities will need to be considerably adjusted.

Setting up standard procedures for removing and replacing shoes and socks makes this task much easier. Establish a designated place in the room to put shoes (with socks tucked inside). This might be each child's cubby or shoes can be neatly lined up against a wall. Avoid having them left in a pile, because that will make retrieval chaotic. As soon as children have placed their shoes and socks, they may go directly to a designated starting place (such as the circle.)

Procedures for retrieving shoes at the end of class should be planned as well, to avoid a confusing scene. Some suggestions include:

1.   Dismiss students by two's or three's to get their shoes and return to the circle to put them on. (If they stay in the shoe area, they will block access for others.)

2.   Carry several pairs of shoes at a time around the circle, allowing each child to claim his or her own.

3.   Decide on a nonverbal signal children may give you if they need help with shoes and socks. (For example, they may sit with both legs outstretched.)

All of the above—space, scheduling, numbers, and dress—are relative "constants." There is another factor that you will always have to consider, but it is not at all stable; we might call it the "environment of the day." If you are an experienced teacher, you are well aware of how one day the children may feel scattered, and the next day settled. While much of this change is still a mystery, there are factors you can become aware of and then make allowances for as you plan a session. Some of these include the weather (the first snowy day, rising or falling barometric pressure, or the fifth rainy day in a row); excitement of other anticipated events (birthday celebration, field trip, impending holidays); or a TV special on late the night before. You will find other events that will influence the environment of the day, but you will still be surprised on many occasions. (See Chapter 6 for some suggestions on dealing with these times.)

SETTING THE GROUND RULES

Part of the preparation you must do as you begin any new activity is with the children, setting up the ground rules that are essential for the activity to happen without disaster. These need not be presented as a heavy-handed lecture, but can be tried out in a spirit of adventure and enjoyment. Of course, just because children hear the rules once does not mean they will assimilate them; rather, you must give children a chance to try them on until they become internalized. Some essential ground rules are as follows.

1.   There will be times for making noise and times for being quiet and still.

Teaching Idea: Making Noise and Making Silence

Concept: Ground Rules

Activity: Give the children a signal for making noise—perhaps holding arms and hands up—and a signal for making silence—perhaps hands down on the floor. Give them several opportunities to practice responding to the signals. As the children are making noise, they will also be doing some movement; as they make silence, they will be fairly still. So, next expand this element so that wiggling around goes with making noise and a *freeze* is part of the silence.

Teaching Note: Total stillness is a beautiful "sound." Point it out so the children will "hear" the silence just as they hear sound.

At the beginning of your teaching, you may find it helpful to establish a signal such as a drum beat for stillness and quiet, which can be heard over noise. (If so, be prepared to spend some time introducing the drum itself, giving the children a chance to play it; occasionally, a younger child may be frightened by the sound.) Later, such a loud signal will become practically unnecessary. Once you give the signal, wait for the children to listen and reach stillness before you begin to speak. It generally does no good to continue pounding on a drum over and over to try to get attention; this will just teach children that they may ignore the signal the first time.

2. Stay in the dancing space. (This needs to be established before the children begin to move through space.)

This point is unnecessary if you are working in a completely empty room that is just the right size. In many cases, however, you will be working in a cleared section of the classroom, a room that is too large, or one that contains some items that are off limits. By defining the "dancing space," you can avoid problems of children running into the far corners, hiding under tables, and other wonderful games they love to play. At this time, call attention to any other safety factors in your environment.

Teaching Idea: Establishing the Dancing Space

Concept: Ground Rules

Activity: While the children watch, walk and/or "paint" an imaginary "boundary line" to indicate the boundaries you wish them to acknowledge. Define the inside area as the Dancing Space. Then, go to different spots in the room, both inside and outside the boundaries, and ask "Am I in the dancing space?"

Teaching Note: You may also wish to establish a "watching place" for children to quietly observe if they choose not to participate.

---

3. There will be no bumping into each other; each person's individual space must be respected, whether they are sitting in a circle or moving through space.

Some teachers like to introduce the concepts of "personal space" and "shared space". In introducing this rule, *personal space* is the space an individual is occupying; *shared space* is the overall space in which all are dancing. Another popular way to introduce this ground rule is to tell children to get inside their own "spacebubble" to dance, and that they must not pop each others' bubbles. However, I have found that many preschoolers think popping imaginary bubbles is a great deal of fun.

Teaching Idea: Moving Without Bumping

Concept: Ground Rules

Activities:
  (a) While sitting in a cluster or circle, ask the children if they can find ways to move their hands and arms without touching someone else. Try it with other body parts.
  (b) Ask the children if they are ready to try something very hard—everyone walking at the same time, without bumping into anyone else. Ask the children how they will do it, or demonstrate moving carelessly and ask the children if that will work.
  Also try this activity using different kinds of traveling movements.

Teaching Note: If you have many children in a small space, delay traveling through space for everyone at the same time until they have more experience and success with maintaining concentration while moving in place.

CULTIVATING THE MAGICAL

This is probably the most significant aspect of preparing children to dance. In order for children to understand that dancing is different from just everyday "moving around," you must cultivate their awareness of the magical quality whenever it occurs. Make sure that children understand you are not talking about magic *tricks* like magicians do, but about a special and *real* feeling.

You will find many opportunities for this, both before and after you begin dance sessions. Some suggestions include:

1. Have a quiet time for listening to special sounds. The children can close their eyes while you produce sounds from objects around the classroom. Also ask the children to listen for the silences.

2. Bring in special objects to see and/or touch. Pass them around with the sense of awe and care they deserve.

3. Whenever you discover something magical outdoors (the shell from a robin's egg, a spider's web covered with dew) point it out to the children in a quiet and respectful way.

4. Read to them from books suggested on page 150, as well as others you find that emphasize magical quality in an experience.

5. Tell children about times when *you* feel magical inside, and encourage them to tell you about times they feel magical—perhaps waking up early in the morning, when it is very quiet, or looking at a lighted Christmas tree in the dark.

When you are ready to begin leading dance sessions, it is helpful to start out by exploring what dancing feels like, compared to other ways of moving. Even once children understand how to find their magic, it is usually necessary to have periodic review.

Teaching Idea: Finding Magic Inside

Concept: Establishing a Sense of *Dance*

Activity: Select an everyday movement, such as standing up and sitting down. Try doing it so it feels "plain and ordinary," and then so it feels silly. Then do it so it feels magical inside. Repeat.

Other movements can be added to this simple beginning to make a sequence, for example, Rise up—turn—run—freeze—sink down. Again, do it with and without "magic."

Teaching Note: The accompaniment you choose and the sound of your voice are important factors in helping children find their magic.

Despite the emphasis here on a wonderful magical quality, it is important to remember that children cannot sustain this quality—and the concentration it demands—indefinitely. When you see the magic beginning to fade and other feelings beginning to erupt, it is important to give space for these, too, so that you will not "lose" the children and their ability to reenter this special realm. See Chapter 5 for a discussion of responding to children's feelings in conducting a session.

REVIEW

1. Considerations in planning
   - Finding the best space—size, arrangement, safety, distractions, aesthetics
   - Choosing the best time
   - Selecting the most appropriate number of children
   - Dressing for dance

2. Establishing ground rules
   - Times for noise and times for stillness and quiet
   - Defining boundaries
   - Respecting individual space

3. Cultivating the magical

CHAPTER 4

Planning
a Dance Session

Once you have made general preparations for dance in your school, you are ready to begin planning a session. The first question teachers ask is, of course, "What will I teach?" Once you have established the ground rules and made the other preparations suggested in Chapter 3, you can actually "begin anywhere."

I usually spend my first two dance sessions with children working primarily with material from Level I (see Chapter 2). I introduce them to the idea of moving with magic to make dance and teach them the concepts of freeze, body shape, and shaping. However, material in dance is not a series of stair steps, each of which must be mastered before moving on to the next. Rather, each concept or element is related to every other, and any starting place can lead to all of the other places. You can begin with any material with which children can become fully involved.

In teaching older children, I often base an individual session on a particular movement concept, bringing it to the students' awareness so that they may incorporate it into their "dance vocabulary." For example, an entire session may be based on *levels*, and all or almost all of the activities will be designed to develop an in-depth understanding of the concept. The session usually culminates with a created dance using levels, which allows children to "pull together" the work of the whole session. This kind of structure tends to be less appropriate for preschoolers than for older children, both because young children's potential for development of skills and concepts is more limited and because of the limits of their attentiveness. However, some movement concepts can lead to a series of movement activities very appropriate for preschoolers, allowing them to work for a whole session with one major concept. An example of such a session, based on curved and straight lines, may be found in Appendix E.

I think of the structure of a typical preschool class as rather like "beads on a string," in which a succession of different movement concepts is explored, one after the other, to whatever depth is suitable at that particular moment. This kind of development, however, is not just a collection of unrelated activities. The concepts may add to each other, perhaps culminating in a final sequence, such as Run—Twirl—Stretch—Fall. The movement concepts may also be tied together by an overall theme that is movement-related. The theme may be an idea (such as *fire, balloons,* or *feelings*) or may be based on a story, poem, or song. Working with movement related to a theme that interests preschool children is one of the most successful ways to work with this age child, and this is the format on which I will concentrate here.

The actual process of planning a session has five steps:

1. Choosing a theme.

2. Brainstorming.

3. Developing activities.

4. Planning the flow of the session.

5. Planning for space and materials.

CHOOSING A THEME

In choosing a theme, there are several things to think about. First, the material should excite you as a teacher as well as be meaningful to the children, based on their experiences. Perhaps this is one reason why seasonal themes tend to work very well. In the peak of autumn, both the children and I feel excited about leaves and the way they hang, drift, and fall. Holidays are another obvious choice, as are special events (such as the circus). Do consider the potential interest of your students in whatever theme you select. I remember a wonderful session I led for 5- and 6-year-olds, dealing with the theme of *teeth* (crooked and straight, pointed and curved, wiggling and falling, biting and chewing); this theme was of great significance to children losing teeth. However, the same material was of little interest to 3- and 4-year-olds, as I promptly found out!

Another important consideration is that the theme should be full of movement possibilities—movement and shape words should come readily to mind when you think about it. It is probably possible to dance about almost anything, but some ideas are more limited than others. A theme of "fruits and vegetables," for example, would probably have more possibilities for a sensory awareness session than for a movement session. Some themes involve movement that is mostly pantomime, and they are, therefore, harder to extend to dance. For example, *getting dressed* involves zipping, buttoning, tying, etc. However, all of these movements are so specific that it is harder, though not impossible, to open them up to movement with more possibilities. In choosing such a theme, you will have to stretch your imagination beyond the usual and think of such things as tying yourself into a knot or buttoning your hand to your knee.

It also is important to look at the values you are reinforcing in your selection. I am particularly concerned with trying to avoid stereotypes. This does not mean that I cannot choose *Indians* as a theme, but that I must be very *sensitive* as to how I develop it. The stereotype of the "Indian war dance" does nothing to help children appreciate the richness of the Native American heritage. Some preschool children may be very interested in dramatic play about superheroes; since this play tends to be very movement-oriented, you may think this is an appealing theme for children. I choose not to encourage this kind of play, as it seems to bring out violence and aggression and limit a child's imagination to the kinds of story lines seen on television.

You may think right away of animals as thematic material since they do indeed move and they are of great interest to preschoolers. There are, however, severe limitations as to how creative children will be if you tell them to "be a cat" or "be a butterfly." This kind of direction tends to produce very stereotyped responses. While it is fun for children to walk around on hands and knees saying "meow," and this is part of their natural dramatic play, they can cheerfully move beyond this level of response. Does this mean that you cannot deal with animals as thematic material? No, but it does mean that, if you choose animals as a theme, you will need to be very imaginative in thinking of the kinds of motion an animal can do when you begin the brainstorming stage of planning. A cat, for example, can stretch, arch its back, curl into a ball, jump straight up, and land softly, among other things. A butterfly can change directions suddenly, hover in the air, and rest lightly on one spot after another.

Even when I work with animals as thematic material, I do not ordinarily ask children to pretend to be any animal—or, for that matter, to be the wind or a melting candle, either. This is not only because it is limiting (there are many ways to jump besides the way a rabbit jumps) but because dance should help us see beyond movement that is ordinary and expected. I do offer children images of animal movement, using them to extend their own movement possibilities. For example, I might say, "The frog's tongue darts out *suddenly* to catch a fly. Can you dart suddenly with your tongue . . . your hand . . . your leg . . . Can you suddenly open and close your eyes? . . . Try another *sudden* motion with a small part of your body."

There are times, of course, when children are already pretending, such as when a child says "I'm a frog today. Ribet!" At such times, you may wish to enter the fantasy with the child, gradually working toward more open possibilities. ("Suppose you were a magic frog who didn't want to jump like all the other frogs . . .").

By now, you probably have many ideas for themes. Appendix B contains a listing of some I have found especially rich for working with preschoolers.

BRAINSTORMING

Once you have selected your general theme or major concept(s), the next task is to brainstorm related ideas in movement terms. This means thinking of everything you know about the subject that could translate into motion and/or shape. At this point, do not stop to worry about *how* you might actually present activities to preschoolers; instead, just write down everything you think of. Let's look at two different themes and some of the ideas we might come up with.

Theme: *Snow*

Snow itself:

Falling
Covering
Blowing/Drifting
Melting
Softness (as snow), hardness (as ice)
Snowflakes, icicles, snowballs (shapes)

People in the snow:

Shivering
Rolling (snowballs)
Throwing, dodging
Leaving footprints and bodyprints (snow angels)

Poems about snow:

"First Snow"—Marie Louise Allen
"The More It Snows"—A. A. Milne

Books about snow:

The Snowy Day—Ezra Jack Keats

Theme: *Baking Bread*

Sprinkling yeast
Stirring until it softens
Mix in other ingredients . . . gets stiffer
Kneading
Rising
Punching down
Letting dough rest
Shaping it
Baking (rising, getting hard on outside)

Books about bread baking:

In the Night Kitchen—Maurice Sendak

These lists do not represent a complete collection of movement ideas for each theme; hopefully, you will think of some ideas I didn't!

After you have a list of ideas, you are ready to develop them into movement activities.

DEVELOPING ACTIVITIES

As you were brainstorming, you were probably beginning to get some pictures in your mind of your children doing the movement. In the next planning step, you will really begin to imagine yourself leading a session and your children responding. This step is actually three steps:

1.   Translating your idea (from the theme) into a *movement concept* or concepts.

2.   Planning an *exploration of the movement concept* (finding different ways to move that fulfill the concept).

3.   Planning a *structure for a dance*, in which children can use the movement they discovered during the exploration.

I will discuss these one at a time. The process may sound cumbersome and intimidating but, with a little experience, it will become quite intuitive. Then, planning will take *much* less time.

Translating the Idea into Movement Concepts

Look at each one of your thematic ideas and try to figure out what movement concepts are involved. Some of these are self-evident, such as falling or rising. Others may require that you turn back to Chapter 2 to see where the idea "fits."

There certainly is room for interpretation here, so do not be too concerned if you are not certain about your choice. I decided to explore the movement concepts of pushing and turning (nonlocomotor movement) under the thematic idea of kneading; you might just as well decide to explore strength. It is important, though, to find at least one movement concept that each of the thematic ideas is about. If you cannot find one, you will probably wish to drop that idea for now.

Planning the Exploration

Next, try to imagine how you and the children can explore the meaning of the concept—not in abstract terms, of course, but as concrete movements. During the exploration of a concept, children will start becoming acquainted with it and discovering its possibilities (some have more possibilities than others). This is just what you will do as you plan.

It is especially important to free yourself from your usual ways of thinking about the movement, because everyday movement often does not go beyond pantomime to become *dance*. Translating the idea into movement concepts helps; thinking about sprinkling as light tapping movements keeps you from being "stuck" into imagining only sprinkling yeast into a bowl with your hands! It also helps to change some of the other aspects of the movement that are ordinarily associated with the everyday action. For example, could you sprinkle up high or down low (levels)? Could you sprinkle with your toes or other body parts (body parts)? Could you sprinkle behind yourself (relationship)? Try sprinkling in a circle (pathways). Could you sprinkle the whole floor by using your whole self, perhaps jumping or tiptoeing (locomotor movements)? What other ways could you find to sprinkle?

These are the kinds of questions and suggestions you will present to your children as you explore the movement idea. I usually begin with more specific suggestions ("Try it with your feet") and then move toward more open-ended ones ("Can you do it with a different part?" "Try it another way.") Of course, you will not plan for all the suggestions to come from the teacher; as we shall see in Chapter 5, you will also be using suggestions from the children.

In order to help children explore more deeply and experience the ongoingness of movement, you will often need to improvise some accompaniment during the exploration. Without accompaniment, children do not know to continue moving or when to stop. While more experienced students can follow directions to "begin when you are ready" and "finish when the movement has come to an end," young children moving in a group need clear signals.

Accompaniment during the exploration usually consists of voice and/or improvised rhythm on a drum or other instrument. The most valuable musical instrument you possess is your own voice. You may be saying to yourself, "Not me! I can't sing." I used to think the same thing; I failed to make the fourth grade chorus, and never took vocal music beyond the sixth grade because I was told I "couldn't sing!" I share this personal anecdote to give you extra encouragement to try. Your voice is always available, never needs plugging in, and can respond instantly to what the children are doing. As you are singing, you can include children's names, directions for making an action bigger or bringing it to a finish—and help emphasize the magical quality you are seeking. The song you sing does not have to rhyme and, if pitch is a problem, you can do more of a chant, such as

slow-ly grow-ing in- to a shape and freeze it.

An instrument may add to your voice to extend possibilities, but can never replace it for working with young children.

Once you are experienced, you will be able to improvise accompaniment for exploration in dance without prior planning. As you begin, however, you will probably need to plan and practice it while an imaginary group of children dances.

To summarize, the exploration is a time to get acquainted with a particular movement and some of its possibilities. The theme you are working with should be thought of as a jumping off point, not as a limitation.

Planning a Dance Structure

Even with accompaniment, the exploration sometimes feels more like problem solving in movement; the next logical—and important—step is to provide a structure in which children can do more extended dancing with the particular movements they have discovered (and will continue to discover). At this point, you will help them create *a dance*. Some form is necessary in order to make *dancing* become *a dance*. However, at the preschool level, *a dance* is not a complex combination of steps done exactly the same way each time. It is, rather, a structure on which children can improvise, so the dance is being created at the same time that it is being performed.

To structure a dance on the preschool level, you need only four things:

1.   An idea for the dance to be about, one that involves several movement possibilities.

2.   A beginning.

3.   Accompaniment to keep the dance going.

4.   An ending.

Let's look at these one at a time.

The *idea* for the dance is simple—it is the same as you used in the exploration. If you explored movement concepts involved in *sprinkling*, for example, you can then do a "sprinkling dance." Often, you will want to explore several movement ideas and then combine them into one dance, such as a dance involving soft running, soft falling, and spreading out to make a covering shape. (See the sample lesson using a *snow* theme.) If you choose to make a dance involving more than one kind of movement, you will also need to let children know when to change from one to the next: Will you give them a signal, or will they pick their own time to change? (The latter is difficult for preschoolers.) During your planning period figure out:

• At what points (following which explorations) during the class children might make a dance based on the structure you give them.

- What you might say to introduce the idea of the dance. (It can be very simple, such as "Now let's do a sprinkling dance, so you can use some of your favorite ways to sprinkle.")

The *beginning* sets off the dance from "everyday" movement; having a clear beginning helps children distinguish when they are dancing and when they are not. A definite beginning also heightens the children's awareness of the wonderful moment of expectation when "dance is about to begin." I ordinarily ask for a moment of stillness, encouraging the children to pay attention to what their muscles feel like just before they start dancing and how the air feels. This request needs to be delivered, not as a heavy-handed "QUIET!" but with a magical voice to encourage the wonder of the moment. During your planning time, imagine how you might begin the dance.

Once the dance begins, you need to have a way to keep it going. Experienced dancers may complete an entire dance in silence, but beginners of any age ordinarily need some sort of *accompaniment* to support the movement and sustain their involvement. As in the exploration, you may often use only your voice and a simple instrument to accompany a dance. However, at some point during a class, you will want to use music. Unless you are or have access to a musician, this means using recorded music. Appendix A contains a number of specific suggestions for selecting and using recorded music. During your planning time, select the music you will use for the dance session. Try it out and then label it so you will have it ready for immediate use; if you are using taped music, wind the tape to the beginning.

The *ending* for a preschool dance involves a freeze or some other way to stop the movement (such as melting down to the floor). You may signal the ending in a variety of ways; for example, your song may end in a direction to "Freeeeeze it," the drum may make one louder beat and stop, and/or you may stop the music on the phonograph. By watching the children, you will usually be able to tell when it is the right time to end a dance (see Chapter 5). It is important that the children know when the dance is finished, even if each child is choosing his or her own time to end it. I often say, "Relax now" or, "Turn yourself into a plain ordinary person instead of a magical one" so that it will be clear to children when we are dancing and when we are not.

It is often difficult to plan the ending of a dance in advance. For now, as you are practicing your accompaniment, also practice an ending. Let's summarize this step of the planning process:

- Translate your ideas into movement concepts.

- Imagine leading an exploration—think of questions and suggestions you could offer the children to help them discover different movement possibilities within the concept.

- Look for points at which a dance may be created from movement discovered during an exploration—imagine a beginning, select and practice accompaniment, and imagine an ending.

Throughout your practicing, remember that how you use your voice is as important as what you say. So, practice with a voice that will encourage the quality you hope will be present in the children!

By the time you reach this point, you will probably have decided that some of your initial ideas are not fruitful in terms of movement or that you have too many for one session. You may add, discard (and perhaps save for another session), or combine ideas at any time!

PLANNING THE FLOW

Just as you are concerned that each individual activity be satisfying, you should also try to be sure that the way that different activities "fit together" will create an overall satisfying session and a feeling of wholeness. It is often helpful to think of entire sessions in several different stages.

The Initial Transition

The first stage you must plan for is a transition from the previous activity(ies) to dance. The children may well have been scattered throughout the classroom, pursuing individual and small-group interests. If so, your task will be similar to what you ordinarily face at "circle time": to reestablish the cohesiveness of the group and the bonding of the group to the leader. At the same time, the children need a chance to settle in and focus their energies in a new direction. If the children are already accustomed to coming together in a circle or cluster to receive directions or to change activities, your task will be easier. In some schools, there is a standard signal, such as a gentle bell that means, "Stop what you are doing and listen." (Whistles do not work very well—they always break a magic spell!)

There are many ways to achieve this transition; some may be directly related to the session to follow, although this is not always necessary. The simplest way is a conversation or discussion directed by the teacher. Other teacher-directed activities, such as songs and finger plays, may be appropriate. At other times, music might draw the group together, or children might focus on a new object—perhaps a flower or a picture that may serve as an introduction to the theme for the class. A more unusual but often very successful way is for you to "perform"—to dance, play an instrument, or say a poem. Sometimes, depending on the state the children are in, you may need to do a very vigorous transition or a relaxation exercise (see Chapter 6). You probably have used many other means of getting on the same wavelength with the children. It simply is important not to get into the session until the children are ready. If the children are *not* ready for dance, it is usually much better to do something else.

If your children move to another space for dancing, this relocation can serve as a transition. Children learn readily to enter the dancing space, remove their shoes and socks (and put them in a designated place), and sit down on a taped circle.

Part of the transition may also include "finding your magic." This may mean a moment of sitting with eyes closed or making some small movement (such as quivering the hands) that children come to associate with the magical quality of dance.

The Introduction

Next, introduce the theme or concept, the working idea for the session. While sometimes it is relevant to review what they did in the previous dance session, preschoolers tend to be much more interested in what they will be doing *today*. The introduction is more than just a statement of what you plan to do; it is connecting the subject to the children, lighting a spark, making the idea seem wonderful and fascinating to them. Again, there are many ways to achieve this goal—you may wish to present an object or picture, a song, poem, story or music, even special food, or a change of lighting. I prefer to keep this stage rather brief with preschoolers and/or to combine it with the initial transition since they are easy to motivate and usually ready to get into action. I most frequently use a simple statement or share a thought or experience (real or imaginary).

With a fairly small group, asking questions (i.e., "Have you ever baked bread before?") may be a good way to draw the children to the material; however, there are some possible pitfalls in this approach. Since preschoolers tend to be most interested in their *own* story, you may end up with all talk and no time for moving, with each child having a pressing need to relate his or her own lengthy story. Before you ask a question, think about what answers you might expect from preschoolers! Also, the questioning approach should not be used unless you are interested in their answers; do not let it become a game of "20 Questions" for the children to guess the one idea you are thinking of (i.e., "What do you make with flour and yeast?").

The introduction ends when interest is high and the children are ready to enter into the magic with you.

Arrange Activities in Logical Order

Next in your planning, arrange the activities in a logical order. There are two main aspects to consider here. One relates to what we may call the dynamics of the class, or how you get variety so that children will not lose interest. You should alternate between very vigorous activities and quieter ones; include a balance between activities that require a great deal of concentration and those that require less concentration. Try not to plan three body parts activities in a row. Try to anticipate when the children will need a change of pace.

The second aspect has to do with the organization of the class as a group of individuals sharing space. I have found that the general pattern of organization that works best in my classes involves beginning close together and gradually moving out to use the larger space. I most frequently begin the class with children gathered together in a circle for a guided exploration. All of the children will move at the same time in their own space, most often working in some way with isolated body parts. If they are well focused, they can begin with small movements and/or smaller body parts. If the children are more wound up, they will need to begin with larger muscle movement and more vigorous action (also see Chapter 6).

As their energy builds and activities require more space, we move out so the children have their own spot on the floor. At first, and perhaps even for some time with a large or young group, the children need help distributing themselves so that they are evenly scattered rather than in a clump. You may lead each child to a given spot, or even carry them there while they are in a favorite shape. We then generally begin activities that can be done in that one spot; I want to be sure that the children are "with me" before they begin to move through space. After you have worked with children for some time, and they really understand the ground rules, this stage will move quickly.

Following this stage, I tend to follow different patterns depending on the size of the class and the size of the room. In a very large group (25 or more), children usually stay in their given spot for the rest of the class, moving within that general space (or leaving it and returning to it). When I first faced the challenge of teaching a group of 35 in a classroom barely large enough, I was amazed at how many different ways we could move without traveling through space! (I did, however, give the children a chance to dance more freely—in smaller groups—before the session ended.)

In a medium-sized group (15 to 25 students), children can alternate in-place movement with much more free movement through space, returning to a cluster around the teacher when necessary to reestablish the sense of group or to receive new directions. In a smaller group, the children will have more opportunity to move through space and make individual contributions to the class. This situation is, of course, ideal.

This "small-to-large" pattern of organization—like most of the suggestions in this book—should be considered a helpful guideline rather than an ironclad rule. If a different kind of organization works for you, then use it. The smaller and/or more experienced the group, the more flexibility you will have. Your experience, too, will make a difference in terms of how much structure you give a class.

You have probably already considered the beginning and ending of each activity; you may need to adjust these so you can move smoothly from one activity to the next, and think about what transitions, verbal or otherwise, will be needed. For example, if the children have just run through space and then melted to the floor, they will be scattered about the room. If you need them to be close together for the next activity, you will need to find a way to get them there.

I try to include at least one time in each class when I touch every child. This has become important to me in maintaining my connection to each individual, and has become important to the children as well, so that they frequently find ways to request such moments. ("The shirts need ironing . . . iron us by *touching* us," a child told me once, in the middle of our "laundry dance.") There are many opportunities for this to occur within activities (checking to see if the body is tense or relaxed, for example), but transitions between activities also offer times for transporting a child in a held shape, as previously discussed, or perhaps a gentle touch on the shoulder as a signal to be "blown by the wind" or to return to the circle.

The Ending

The end of the class should bring the children down from their high level of activity, relax their bodies, and clear their minds for the next event of the day.

During the ending, you may wish to briefly review the material covered; this will help the children retain what they learned. Some common ways to review are:

1.   Ask a different child to demonstrate each kind of movement.

2.   Demonstrate yourself and ask the children to call out the name of the movement.

3. Ask the children to sit quietly as you review the movement words and ideas, and let their muscles remember "inside" what they felt like doing that movement.

4. Ask each child to tell you his or her favorite part of the class.

Some sort of a formal relaxation is especially important to end a very active session. For example, a class dealing with a rain theme might end this way:

> "Lie down on your back, close your eyes, and listen to the rain falling in your mind. See if you can really feel it gently falling on your arms, legs, head, . . .
> Let all the feelings get washed out of you now, so you are really empty and floppy and can start with new fresh feeling for something we'll do next. . . ."

Consider where the children will be spatially at the end of the class so you can plan the transition to the next event of the day. You may want them to gather back together or you may dismiss them to another space. It may be time for bathroom visits or putting on coats. It usually will be time to put shoes and socks back on. To avoid a wild scramble for shoes, you may ask children to return to the circle, and bring them their shoes.

Procedures for ending a dance session are very important. One of the nicest "fringe benefits" of dance is the good feeling that can continue for a period of time afterwards—do not let it be destroyed by allowing chaos to erupt! I have often found it helpful to dismiss children to the next activity one at a time, giving them a reminder about appropriate behavior that is in some way related to the session (for example, "Keep that peaceful feeling with you" or "Go as softly as the softest snow").

Planning for Space, Equipment, and Related Curriculum

For most of your sessions, you will need nothing but yourself, your children, empty space, and whatever you need for accompaniment. But now is the time to look over your plans and see if you need to collect any props, books, records, a phonograph or tape player, instruments, or any other equipment. It will be helpful if you have them all together when you are ready to begin.

Probably all the way through your planning you have been aware of other areas of the curriculum to which your lesson connects; perhaps even your choice of theme was determined by this (see Chapter 7). You should be thinking about when related activities will be done—before or after the dance session—and make plans for those as well.

Now, let's look at some actual "lesson plans" based on the two themes we brainstormed earlier. Other sample lesson plans may be found in the Appendix. Remember that *many* different lesson plans can arise from the same theme. Also, as you read these, keep in mind that an actual session almost never goes exactly as planned. How these sessions might actually turn out is discussed in Chapter 5.

Theme: Snow

(Note that this plan involves "adding onto" a sequence, building a longer dance at the end. Such an approach is more appropriate for 4½- to 5-year-olds. The last dance structure would probably not be as successful for younger children.)

1. Introduction: Discussion of weekend's snowfall

2. *Idea*: Snow falling softly

   Concepts: Softness; falling

   Activity: (a) Explore soft sounds (with voice, body parts).
           (b) Explore soft falling (body parts, then whole body).
           (c) Explore soft running through space.
           (d) Dance structure: Run softly; freeze on signal; fall softly. Repeat several times. Last time: children run back to circle and fall very carefully close together, like one big snowdrift.

   Accompaniment: Voice and bell
           "Softly running, softly running, running soft as snow. . . . FREEZE.
           Softly falling, softly falling, falling to the floor."
           (Repeat several times.)

3. Transition: Sit up to look at a picture

4. *Idea*: Snow covering things to make a rounded shape

   Concepts: Covering/spreading out (increasing range); rounded shapes

   Activity: (a) Look at a picture of snow covering cars in a parking lot ("Covering them like a blanket").
           (b) Explore: Spread out slowly to make a covering, rounded shape, then quickly pull in tightly.

   (c) Dance structure (add onto one above): Run softly; freeze; fall softly; spread out slowly to make a rounded shape. Repeat.

Accompaniment: Voice and bell (add on to "song" above.)

5.   Transition: Ask, "How would it feel to be covered up by a pile of snow? You'd need to shake it off; shake yourself very hard—and then shake yourself back to the circle." (Accompany with your voice and drum.)

6.   *Idea*: Snowflake shapes; freezing and melting

   Concepts: Shapes with points and "holes" (negative space); tension and relaxation

Making shapes with points and holes.

   Activity: (a) Show cut-out paper snowflakes. Ask the children what they notice about them. Specifically point out that each snowflake has a different shape, but all have points and many have "holes."
   (b) Explore making shapes with holes and shapes with points; pop into the shapes.
   (c) Explore letting shapes melt and letting them freeze as hard as "ice."

(d) Dance structure: Run freely through space; at signal, choose whether to freeze hard into a shape with holes and points, or to melt down to the floor.

Accompaniment: Drum

7. Transition: "Now we are going to make a magical dance about snow. Let's start our dance together over here."

8. *Idea*: Dance about snow

Concepts: (Combining previous concepts of session)

Activity: (a) Dance structure: Soft running; freeze; fall softly to make a covering rounded shape; pop into a hard shape with holes and points; repeat several times. Last time: Snowflake shapes get blown back to the circle where they melt into a puddle of water.

Accompaniment: Record: "Snowflakes Are Dancing," plus verbal cues for each section.

9. Ending:
    (a) Review: Ask the children to make a picture in their minds of the parts of the dance, as you call them out.
    (b) Relaxation: All children lie on the floor, making themselves soft and heavy. Check each child individually to make sure each one is completely relaxed. Dismiss them individually to put on shoes, with a reminder to move "softly as the snow."

Equipment needed:

Phonograph

Record, *Snowflakes Are Dancing* ((Tomita) ERCA, ARL 1-0488)

Pictures (1) Snow covering cars
         (2) Snowflakes (cut out of paper)

Drum

Bell

Theme: Baking Bread

1. Introduction: Discussion about bread baking done previous day; recall of steps

2. *Idea*: Sprinkling yeast

Concepts: Light tapping; relationships

Activity: (a) Discuss yeast as a magic "ingredient" that makes bread rise.
(b) Explore light tapping movements, discovering different places to "sprinkle" (in front of, behind, to the side, above, below).

3. *Idea*: Stirring

   Concept: Circular pathways; body parts

   Activity: (a) Pantomime stirring to discover a circular pathway.
   (b) Explore making circular pathways with different body parts.
   (c) Dance structure (combining two ideas):
   Song:
   Soft voice: "Find a place to sprinkle,
   lightly, lightly sprinkle. . ."
   Big voice: "Now stir it up, stir it up,
   Stir it up, stir it up"
   (Continue)
   Last line: "Now it's time to freeze."

   Accompaniment: Voice and drum

4. *Idea*: Kneading dough

   Concept: Pushing with strength, turning to face a new direction

   Activity: (a) Pantomime kneading to recall pattern.
   (b) Explore pushing against the floor with different body parts; discover how hard muscles must work.
   (c) Practice responding to drum cue by turning to face a new direction when the drum sounds (sort of like a *Simon Says* game).
   (d) Dance structure: Pushing against the floor; using a chosen part; turning to face a new direction when the drum sounds. Repeat.

   Accompaniment: Voice and drum—"Pushing and pushing and pushing *AND TURN*. . . ."

5. Transition: "Now the dough is ready to rise. Pick a spot in the dancing space where you would like to rise; go there and lie down on the floor."

6. *Idea*: Dough rising; punching down dough and letting it rest

Concepts: Slow rising; quick and strong return to low level; relaxation

Activity: (a) Explore: Rising from a low level to a high level, going very slowly and smoothly. (Cue: "Filling up with air.") Going down suddenly and with strength (by pushing the air out, not just falling down).

(b) Dance structure: Slow rising, sudden sinking, and then resting. If possible, let each child choose when to punch down and when to rise again. (Tell the children, "Make sure I can see when you are rising, when you are punching down, and when you are resting.")

Accompaniment: "Music for Things that Are Quiet"

7. *Idea*: Shaping the dough, baking

Concept: Shapes; degrees of tension

Activity: (a) Ask: "What if we discovered magic dough that could put itself into different shapes?"

(b) Explore making different shapes.

(c) Explore making the shapes just barely hard enough to hold their shapes—soft like unbaked dough. Then explore making them a little harder, like bread feels when it comes out of the oven ("with a crust on the outside, but soft inside").

8. Transition: "When all the shapes are baked, I'll put them over on this side of the room. Hold your shape just hard enough so that it will not fall apart when I pick you up."

9. *Idea*: (Story) While the bread cools, the baker takes a nap and all of the breads "magically" start to dance.

Concept: Free choice of movement to music

Activity: (a) Tell the story: A baker leaves all of his bread shapes out to cool while he goes to take a nap in the back of the shop. While he sleeps, the bread shapes come to life and start to dance, dancing about all of the kinds of movement used in baking bread: sprinkling, stirring, kneading, rising and punching down, resting, and making shapes. They dance so much they turn into dancing children. By the time the baker wakes up, all he sees are *children* sitting in a circle; the bread has disappeared. To this day, the baker doesn't know where his bread went on that magical day, but now he has a lot of helpers in the bakery.

(b) Dance structure: All the children begin in their "baked" shape, while the "baker" (the teacher) checks each one. Then the "baker" takes a "nap" (next to the record player). While the music plays, the children dance freely. (Probably only the 4½- to 5-year-olds will remember many of the movements from earlier in the session. The "baker" can "talk in his [or her] sleep" to remind them.) Near the end of the music, suggest quietly that they all sneak back to the circle and sit there like they do at circle time. Then the "baker" wakes up and acts appropriately astonished.

Accompaniment: "Dance of the Sugar Plum Fairy," from *The Nutcracker Suite*

10. *Ending*: Ask the children if they can remember how to make their muscles as soft as soft dough. Then ask them to make their muscles just hard enough so they can go to get their shoes.

Equipment:
Drum
Phonograph
Records: "Music for Things that Are Quiet," from *Adventures in Rhythms*, Ruth White. (Rhythms Productions CC 623) "Dance of the Sugar Plum Fairy," from *The Nutcracker Suite* (any recording).

This degree of planning—involving many levels and much time—seems enormously cumbersome, and indeed it is at first, when you need to plan for every possibility. Eventually, just like other skills, it will become practically automatic. Extensive planning will become much less significant once the elements of movement are second nature to you and you have an intuitive feel for the children and what you can expect from them (and they from you!). At that point, your plan will be a mere skeleton of ideas, filled in by the children, as you will be confident of your ability to take their contributions and structure them to make them work. The next chapter deals with that process.

REVIEW

1. Choosing a theme

2. Brainstorming

3. Developing activities
   - Translating ideas into movement concepts
   - Planning an exploration of the movement concepts, including accompaniment
   - Planning dance structure, including accompaniment

4. Planning the flow, including introduction, transitions, and ending

5. Planning for space and materials

CHAPTER 5

Conducting
the Class

Once you have prepared a complete lesson plan, you have made a considerable investment. Your ideas are marvelously creative, well suited to your children, and arranged in a logical order. You are probably rather attached to the whole thing. This attachment is the biggest danger of all, because your job in conducting the class will be to connect not to your lesson plan, but to the children—who almost never respond just as you expect them to. Connecting to the children does not mean putting a lesson plan on a group. However, neither does it mean children just doing anything they want.

There are two major ways that you connect to children in the class. One is by responding to their *ideas* and *feelings*. Another is by using your *energy* appropriately. Both of these aspects will be discussed in this chapter. We will also look at the evaluation process in teaching dance to preschool children.

IDEAS AND FEELINGS

The class itself operates on two interrelated levels: *ideas* and *feelings*. The *ideas* we are especially interested in during a dance session relate to movement (the concepts discussed in Chapter 2) and/or the content (theme) of the session. We notice a child's ideas—and share our own—through both words and actions. For example,

A teacher may say, "Can you make a shape with points?" or
A child may stick out two fingers and his or her tongue.
A child may say, "Sometimes snow gets hard, not soft" or
A teacher may demonstrate making muscles hard.

You worked out your ideas during the planning period; now, as you lead the session, be very observant of children's ideas. It will be very helpful if you practice observing children's movement, so you can recognize readily what you see:

- What body parts are being used (what parts are moving and what parts are supporting weight).
- Identifiable movements (rolling, wiggling, pushing, twisting).
- Aspects of space, time, energy, and relationship.

You may want to spend some time just watching children move on the playground, naming to yourself what they are doing.

Feelings are also revealed through words and actions. For example,

A child may very tentatively demonstrate use of a new body
part, looking around anxiously at what others are doing.
A teacher may say, "I never thought of that before."
A child may interrupt the teacher to say, "I know how to do it!"
A teacher may give a disapproving look.

Children—and adults—reveal feelings at the same time they express ideas (with confidence, shyness, boredom) as well as at other times during a session. It may be harder to tell what someone is feeling than what body part they are using, but we all have some skill at "reading" children's feelings—through observing their faces, bodies, and movement as well as by listening. Despite all of the attention given to ideas in the previous chapter, a session can never work without giving much attention to feelings.

INTERACTION

Both ideas and feelings serve as the material for *interaction*, the process through which the class is conducted. We may think of interaction as a series of connected and related responses between the children and the teacher. It is a give and take relationship in which teachers and children respond to each other. The teacher is not always "the boss," but neither are the children. Maintaining interaction in a session is important for several reasons. Anyone who has worked in a creative activity with children knows that their ideas are just as significant as those of adults, and many times are even more imaginative. Too often, we lead children to think that their ideas are inferior to ours; when we use their ideas as well as our own we can help correct this misunderstanding.

An additional reason is very practical—there will be chaos without it. Children are not machines who will do our bidding when we say *jump*; if their needs are not being met, they will find a way to get them met. If children are disinterested or uncomfortable with material we present, or they do not understand, they will tune out and find something more interesting to do, no matter how disruptive that might be.

The process of interaction works like this:

Step 1. The teacher first offers an idea, usually in the form of an activity. This activity may be from the lesson plan, or simply a response to something else the children are doing. For example, you could say, "Can you push hard against the floor with your feet?" or "Try spinning lightly on your bottom."

Step 2. The children respond in movement and sometimes words, expressing their ideas and feelings. Some will do just what you had in mind, but many will not.

The children's responses generally fall into one of three categories:

1. *They may stay with your idea.* In this case, they are following your preplanned expectations from the lesson plan, following directions given, answering questions asked, and finding variations of the original idea. In terms of feelings, there will be believable involvement rather than lethargy, boredom, or hyperactivity.

2. *They may offer a new but related idea.* For example, you might suggest light tapping as a way to experience the idea of sprinkling yeast, and a child may begin to shake a body part instead to capture the sense of sprinkling. As you are working with the idea of stirring, a child may say, "My dad puts eggs in the dough. Let's put eggs in." There will frequently be a spontaneous and rather bursting sense of discovery for the child at this point. You will also notice a real investment of the self; the child's enthusiasm and sincerity at that moment are telling you that you must "go with it." This behavior may be noiser than usual, but the noise is focused and purposeful.

3. *They may drop your idea completely, either for their own ideas or for some degree of chaos.* A different quality and level of noise occurs at these times. The cohesiveness of the group tends to dissolve, with children "doing their own thing" as individuals or in small groups, responding to assorted outside stimuli more than to the teacher. Usually, they will have lost the sense of magical quality and the behavior will look more like "just playing around."

Step 3. The teacher responds to the children. If they stay with your idea, stay with the lesson plan and be alert for additions and expansions the children may make. If there is little variation among the children, you may try to expand the directions, either with more guidance ("Can you find a twisted shape that is upside-down?") or more openness ("See if you can twist into a shape I have never seen before ").

If they offer a new but related idea, develop and structure their ideas as you did with your own during the planning . . . through exploring and forming. ("Justin is sprinkling by shaking—let's try shaking our toes. . ." or "You have to make a hard, quick movement to crack an egg. . . When you hear the drum, can you do a hard, quick movement?")

If they drop your idea completely, it is important to be willing to let it go. Some of the activities children invent to do on their own when they have lost interest are very imaginative; if there are several children involved, it is sometimes possible to bring the group to a new focal point around this activity and go on from there. (You should not, however, feel obligated to develop every idea the children offer; children who continually seem to be on a very different wavelength may simply be indulging in some unique attention-getting behavior, which you may not always want to reinforce.) Otherwise, you can simply acknowledge that your idea was not working and that the children's idea is a very original one. The next step is to reestablish the cohesiveness of the class (which feels like "starting over") and then go on to another item on the lesson plan (or something else that seems more appropriate). It is important to stop the activity before real chaos breaks out, before the children tune you out completely.

It is also important to be aware of why the children have dropped your idea. Many times, children simply cannot stay with a particular kind of quality of movement as long as the teacher expects them to; children have a different sense of timing than adults. Other times, children may be feeling that their own contributions of related ideas are being ignored, and they need to otherwise establish their input to the class. There may be other reasons that have little if anything to do with the session or the teacher. (See Chapter 6 for more specific discussion of some of these situations.)

Step 4. This process of interaction then continues—the children respond, the teacher responds, and so forth.

	Interaction		
Teacher	Offers an idea		
Children Respond	Stay with idea ↓	or Offer a new but related idea ↓	or Drop teacher's idea completely for their own activity ↓
Teacher Responds	Stays with lesson	Develops idea offered	Starts over based on children's activity, or brings children back together for a new beginning

Let's take a look at how the beginning of a session on the theme of snow, so carefully planned in the previous chapter, might really happen, with interaction between the children and the teacher.

Teacher: As you finish putting the toys away, I will play a record about the kind of day it is outdoors—"Winter Wonderland."

Children: (Finish putting toys away and then gather around the teacher)

Teacher: We've been extra noisy in the classroom this morning. I think it's because we haven't had enough good weather to play outdoors recently. I'll bet some of you feel like running and jumping in a snowdrift right now! We don't have room for that kind of running, but can you make a big jump right where you are, without jumping on anyone?

Children: (Respond as expected, with yelling and shrieking)

Teacher: Those were *very* noisy jumps! Can you try making the quietest jump in the world?—and now a big noisy one?—and now a quiet one?

Children: (Respond as expected)

Teacher: Sometimes snow makes me feel like playing hard and being loud, and sometimes it makes me feel quiet and magical inside.

Child: I like to throw snowballs!

Teacher: That's *fun* to do outside, isn't it! But what can we do *inside* with the snow?

Child: Make a mess!

Teacher: You're right. We don't usually bring real snow inside. . .

Child: I do, to make snow cream.

Teacher: Oh, I forgot about snow cream. Except for that, we usually don't—but we can *dance* about snow inside . . . To help us get ready to dance, can you make a sound with your voice, a sound as soft as snow falling?

Child: Snow doesn't make a sound.

Teacher: Maybe it does, but our ears aren't good enough to hear it. Can you make a sound that quietly?

Children: (Respond as expected)

Teacher: That made our classroom feel so magical! Can you clap your hands that softly?

Children: (Respond as expected)

Teacher: How else can you make a soft sound?

Children: (Most respond with soft sounds made by different body parts. One child falls down noisily and others immediately follow.)

Teacher: You're reminding me that it's time for a noisy sound. Let's make a noisy sound, but we'll make it more difficult. *Don't* use your voice.

Children: (Respond as expected)

Teacher: And now the soft sound—
  And now the loud sound—
  And now the soft one—
  Can you stand up and fall down noisily, like Adam?
  Can you fall down as softly as the snow? (Sing "Falling soft
    as *snow.*")

Children: (Most respond with slow, silent falling. One child falls more quickly, making a little noise in the process.)

Teacher: Karen, you made me think of how sometimes a hunk of snow falls down off a branch with a little *plop*—like when the snow is melting on a sunny day. Let's try falling down with a little *plop.*

Children: (Respond as expected)

Teacher: Let's try something. I will play a song on the bells, for light running, and you run as softly and full of magic as you can—as soft as the *most* quiet snow. Then, when the bells stop, you fall down, either gently and softly like snowflakes, *or* with a little plop like a hunk of snow. (Sings and plays)

Lightly running, softly running, quiet as the snow, . . .
Lightly running, softly running, now it's time to fall like snow—

Children: (Running as expected. Children appear confused by the choice in falling.)

Teacher: The running part was so full of magic, but I couldn't tell whether you were falling softly like snowflakes (demonstrate) or with a little plop (demonstrate). Can you try to make it very clear so I will know which one you pick? Decide in your mind which one you will pick . . . Ready, and—(Repeats song)

Children: (Respond as expected)

Teacher: I saw Adam, Karen, Jennifer, Jay, and Melanie fall with a plop, and Michael, Sally, Justin, and Betsy fall like snowflakes. You might pick a different way to fall this time.
(Continues)
And now—(singing)

Lightly running, softly running, over close to me,
Lightly running, softly running
  Gather here by me. . .
(Waits for all children to gather)
And now, let's see if I can close my eyes while you sit down so
  softly I can't hear you. . . .

Children: (Respond as expected)

Teacher: (Shows picture) The snow is covering up the cars like a blanket.

Child: A cold blanket! (Hugs self and shivers)

Teacher: Yes, it makes me cold thinking about it! Let's hug ourselves like
  Sally, and (sing)

shiver shiver shiver
shiver-shiver-shiver
shiver-shiver-shiver and freeze—
and now spread out
to make a covering
rounded shape. . . . (demonstrates while singing)
and now—
shiver-shiver-shiver
in a tight rounded shape
Jennie is even
Making her eyes go
Shiver shiver shiver

(sing):

And now spread out
to make a covering rounded shape—

(Speak): Michael's is like a very thin blanket—

(Continue several times, alternating between the two)—And rest.

Teacher: I guess those are two of the shapes we see on snowy days . . . tight
  shivering shapes and spread out, covering shapes. I have a picture of
  another kind of shape that we can see if we look very closely (shows
  picture of snowflakes).

And the session continues, with teacher and children responding to each
other. Try to give the children confidence to share their ideas by respecting their needs and their feelings and by trying to structure the children's
ideas into activities that will "work" in the context of the session. Sometimes, the planned activities can be adapted to fit the children's re-

sponses, as shown in the example above. Other times, the session may turn out to be completely different. I recall once attempting to lead a session on the theme of baking bread, and it turned out that one child's father was a baker. Jonathan informed me that his father's recipe was quite different, and led us through every step to take!

ENERGY

Another extremely important item to consider in conducting the class is your energy level. The way each of us uses energy is part of our personality as well as teaching style, but we need to be aware of what it is and how to adapt it for successful teaching. Many successful teachers are always "up," bubbling with enthusiasm; just as many move more slowly and quietly, but with assurance and firmness. The most successful teachers, like the most successful dancers, can use their energy differently as the situation demands, to sometimes bring the children up and sometimes settle them down, to lead them in exploding and bursting activities and also relaxation, using the voice and the whole self. The one style that does not work in conducting creative dance is lethargy and passivity. You must be willing to invest considerable energy in a session—not to do all of the activities with the children (although this at times may be appropriate), but to feel their movement as they do it, and give them your total attention and involvement.

It is physically and emotionally wearing to teach preschoolers; teaching dance is even more so. The most significant moments—perhaps the one tentative contribution of the day from one shy child—may pass quickly. You must constantly stay involved and alert to what is happening and what possibilities it holds.

EVALUATION

Another important aspect of conducting sessions is the evaluation process; how are the children doing in dance and how am I doing as leader? As children get older, evaluation becomes more formal—with testing, report cards, etc.—and, unfortunately, more concerned with categorizing people (as not so good, good, better, and best). However, on the preschool level, you can be much more concerned with simply giving immediate feedback to children, helping to develop their self-awareness by sharing with them what you notice. For example, you might say during a day, "You put all of the blue beads in one pile and the red beads in another pile. I wonder what you will do with *these* beads" or "I like the little tiny circles in the corner of your picture." In dance, also, try to describe for children the significant moments you observe: "Your knees look very important in that walk" or "Your whole self looks stretched, all the way through your finger-tips." This is not something else you must do as you watch the class; it merely verbalizes what you are observing and identifying to yourself as you structure the activities of the class.

Children should share in the evaluation process as they begin to notice themselves as well as the group. Whenever children dance individually or in small groups, other children should be encouraged to watch ("See what parts they use") and be given space to make comments. There also are times you might say at the conclusion of an activity or a whole session, "How did that work?" and "Why did it work?" At first, children may not respond at all to these questions, and then only at the level of "Nobody was messing around that time." But, as you continue to reinforce their awareness, helping them to see and giving them a vocabulary for expressing what they see, their awareness will grow. Eventually, a child will realize such things as, "It was exciting because at first it was slow and then there was a fast part" or "I liked the part when only our eyes moved."

Many people use praise as a way of giving feedback, as in "That is a beautiful shape" or "That's a good run." While we usually think of praise as having nothing but positive benefits, sometimes there are negative effects. Frequently, a child may react to an adult's praise by repeating the same behavior over and over, assuming that that way is the only right way. This may be fine when we are trying to shape definite behaviors, but it can be a problem in creative activities when we want a child to continue exploring and finding other ways to move. In addition, when we praise an individual in front of the group, others may well copy (thinking "His must have been the best") or demand reassurance ("Was mine good too?"). If we simply tell children "That's good" without being more specific, they may come to mistrust us, to think we are giving praise without really looking or really meaning it.

While we frequently hear "Everyone needs praise," probably what people need most of all is to be noticed and feel important. Giving children specific feedback about what you observe ("You're moving in such slow motion") and how you feel ("I felt all tingly when I saw you dance"), tells a child he or she is important enough for you to really notice. This of course does not mean that you should never praise a child's efforts, but rather that you should be aware of other means for conveying information and building self-esteem.

When I use my own voice to accompany dance sessions, I often include observational feedback as part of the accompaniment. For example, I might be singing directions for "Painting the air . . . put the paint everywhere" and can include "Joy is using her elbows" or "Jim is painting spots on the floor with his feet."

In addition to giving feedback during the class, I find it helpful to do some evaluation at the end of a session—to rethink the children's response in preparation for planning the next session. I try to notice not only how well the children behaved and enjoyed the session, but also make note of what aspects of movement they were using and not using. If the children do not seem to be using their full range of movement, for example, I might make sure to plan a session that involves stretching. I also try to stay aware of when children may need a review of the basic ground rules.

Another kind of evaluation that is very important for us to do at the end of a session involves reinforcing our own awareness of ourselves as teachers. Some of the kinds of questions I ask myself after a session include:

- Was the subject matter appropriate and presented in an interesting way?

- Did I include a variety of kinds of activities (body parts activities, locomotor and nonlocomotor movement; space, time, and energy variations)?

- Did I *connect* with the children? At what moments did we achieve a truly magical quality?

- Did I overlook important signals (try to continue an activity that children had let go of; ignore good ideas of the children in order to stay with my own)? How could I have responded better?

- What feelings did the children present that I did not know how to deal with? What ideas did they offer that I did not know how to deal with? How could I have handled these? What ideas and feelings did the children present that I responded to very well?

- Did I notice and respond to each child at some point during the session? What in particular did I notice, and what does it tell me about this child and his or her needs?

- Did the session end in a way I felt good about?

- Did I stay truly involved in the session? Did I use my energy appropriately?

- How did I feel about myself during the session?

It is always exhilarating when a session goes very well, and frustrating and discouraging when one does not work. Frequently, you may be able to go back over a session and figure out how you could have done things differently and achieved more success. However, it is important to remember that, no matter how skillful and caring a teacher may be, every session will not always work. Some days there are other events so exciting that it is impossible to compete. Other times, children may bring with them needs you cannot meet within the space of a session—or a whole day or even a whole year. At these times, you may feel as though you have accomplished nothing, as though your efforts were for nought. However, you must keep your perspective—not all seeds will flower during the season they are planted.

CHAPTER 6

Potential Problems
and Some Suggestions
for Handling Them

How often teachers have thought to themselves, "It would have been a great class . . . if it hadn't been for the children!" And yet, of course, teaching children is what we are doing, and children are children, not machines who respond to every button pushed in a predictable way. The days when everything reaches perfection are ones to treasure and nourish us on the days when everything goes wrong.

There are a number of things you can do to help diminish the number of days when everything goes wrong; these have already been discussed in the chapters on planning and teaching. To summarize, they include:

1. Setting clear expectations and ground rules.

2. Choosing material that is of interest to your children.

3. Planning the class carefully and practicing as necessary.

4. Varying the kind of movement used.

5. Using accompaniment to help structure the experience.

6. Responding to the ideas and feelings of children.

7. Using appropriate energy; staying fully involved with the children.

Despite careful planning, however, there will be problems. Some days you can forecast problems and plan for them. Some days children are simply more wound up than others, and you have to use more energy to make the class work.

Many so-called "discipline problems" have a multitude of possible solutions. There are few absolute rules in this area. However, I have found two "rules" of such significance that their violation always brings problems. The first is: NEVER ENGAGE IN A POWER STRUGGLE WITH A CHILD. Always leave a child and yourself a "way out" of a situation so that you both can save face. Do not ridicule or threaten a child, and deal with individual discipline problems privately.

The second rule is: DO NOT ALLOW CHILDREN TO THINK CHAOS IS WORKING. It should be clear by now that dance as described in this book cannot occur in a state of chaos. This does not mean that every activity is quiet and magical but, if children think they are dancing when they are running around screaming, it will be hard to *ever* reach the state of awareness you are seeking. There is sometimes a thin line between freedom and chaos, and each teacher has his or her own standards. However, when an activity is not working, it is important to *say so*—and try to stop it before chaos occurs. If, for some reason, things completely fall apart, do not try to continue with your idea, but instead deal with the immediate problem, which is the chaos.

Instead of blaming the children ("Why can't you ever listen?"), simply label the situation ("This isn't working.") and return to the circle or other position of order. In situations of complete chaos, it will be impossible to pull off an enlightened discussion of why it did not work. The more experience you have, the more skillful you will become at redirecting an activity before it falls apart; then, these times will become rare indeed.

Let's take a look at some of the more frequent behaviors of young children that get in the way of dance, and some possible ways to handle them. Also see the section on disruptive children in Chapter 8 for suggestions on dealing with this kind of problem.

THE NONPARTICIPANT

First of all, *should* everyone actively participate in every session? For a number of years, I operated under the belief that participation should be by choice. As I first started to work with a group, the number of participants would be fairly small, with others choosing to observe or to move to another area; but, by the end of the year, practically every child would be comfortable enough to take part. Then, one year one of the classroom teachers said she would like to begin with the assumption that every child would participate, just as in many other activities; this was communicated to the children, and there was not a single complaint. It reminded me that children accept a great deal without argument when it is presented as a matter of course. At any rate, both methods do seem to result in the eventual involvement of all children.

Different children will have different levels of involvement, as may the same child on different days. When a child is "tuning out," you can encourage greater involvement in a number of ways, such as

Moving closer to the child.

Relocating the child ("Karen, can you move your shape to fill in this empty space?").

Using the child's name in discussion, presentation, or accompaniment.

Making the child an inspiration for an activity ("Michael is lying on his stomach with his elbows touching; can you find a shape to make with your elbows touching the floor?").

If this is not routine behavior for the child, and if there is no response to your initial attempts at encouragement, you may just conclude that the child is taking a "day off," and allow some space for daydreaming. If a child regularly withdraws, not just from dance but from other activities as well, it may be an indication of other problems. See the section on children who are withdrawn in Chapter 8.

If you elect to allow children a choice as to their participation, you must set clear limitations for the nonparticipants. It is very important to maintain an atmosphere in which concentration is encouraged; any interesting noise or activity by their peers can be very distracting for young children. I do not allow anything else to be done in the dancing space, and require that others in the room not disturb. If possible, try to have another adult supervise the nonparticipants so that your attention will not be divided. You may also find ways to include the nonparticipants in the class. (Many of them will be doing the activities with you on the sidelines anyway.)

It is also appropriate to mention the problem of the boy who claims, "This is sissy." The child probably got the idea from a not-too-liberated sibling or father and, fortunately, this sort of attitude is dying out. However, it is important to look at your material and be certain that you are giving the children opportunities to move with strength as well as gentleness, go fast as well as slow, and make twisted, ugly shapes as well as beautiful, curved ones. If a child has this concern, it will also help to direct some particularly challenging activities his way for a while, especially some dealing with strength, balance, coordination, and control.

Moving with strength is a necessary contrast to moving with gentleness.

I have also learned that, just because a child is not actively participating does not mean that the exposure is not having an impact. On several occasions, I have had children who would do nothing more than watch from a distant corner; after months of this I would hear from the parent: "Joey *loves* your class . . . every Wednesday he comes home and shows us everything he did with you in class!" This reminds me that children may have different ways of participating.

CONTAGION

Contagion is usually started by one or two leaders, and suddenly everyone is doing it. Contagious behavior can sometimes be too much for the teacher to turn around; some days you may simply have to say, "It looks like dance is just not going to work today," and then save your wonderful plan for another more favorable day. Many times, however, you can use the mood the children are in and make it work for a very successful class. Below are listed some of the most common kinds of contagious behavior and some possible ways of turning potential disruption into success, usually using the same process of exploring and forming children's ideas. (Beware, however, that some of these behaviors can easily become regular "games" if you encourage them by making them too much fun.) If this kind of treatment does not work, you will need to sit down with the children and admit, "This isn't working," and see if they think they are going to be able to make dance work. (If they say "No," don't try to talk them into it.) You may need to remind them (without scolding) that dancing is magical and that other behavior can keep the magic from happening.

If any of these behaviors occur on a routine basis, something is likely to be more seriously wrong. You will need to look to yourself (sometimes teachers actually encourage these responses by the kind of material they choose and the way they present it) and go back and remind the children of the ground rules.

1.   The sillies (and the giggles)—We all have them at some point, and they are very contagious! Sometimes you can:
  (a) Make a giggle dance, by having one part "giggle," then another part, then another; eventually, the whole self giggles. Try it with and without sound and then collapse and relax. After doing such a dance a few times, the children will usually be ready to go on to something else.
  (b) Use it as a jumping off point to explore feelings . . . make a silly face . . . then a sad face . . . etc. Is *silly* tight or floppy? How about *angry*? Make a silly shape with your whole self . . . an

angry shape, etc. Use plenty of freezes so this will help redirect children instead of winding them up.

2. Excess noise, sound effects (a particular problem when using an image that makes a noise).

    (a) Have the children freeze their bodies so they can put all of their energy into the sound, and then give them an opportunity to make a lot of sound. Then tell them that they will need to stop the sound and give them the directions for moving. Alternate sound and silence several more times. (See the sample session in Chapter 5.)

    (b) Give the children an invitation to make a sound, one so soft that no one else can hear what it is . . . only their secret self, as they move. This often creates an especially high level of concentration; reinforce their awareness of the magical quality it creates.

    (c) Practice a "silent yell" (without any sound coming out). Try a silent yell with other body parts as well. Do the same with other sounds, such as laughing, crying, and whispering.

3. Mass collisions. (This may be contagious behavior, assuming that the space is large enough to avoid this, and the children have demonstrated previously that they can do so.)

Despite the fact that it can be a great deal of fun to bump into people, this usually must be stopped immediately with an appeal to safety ("We cannot dance today if we cannot keep from bumping."). However, if it is just getting started you may be able to ask the children to get as close together as they can without touching ("make yourself very skinny and use your most careful self"), and then as far away as they can without leaving the dancing space. Alternate these two if you feel the children can handle it.

4. Hiding under the tables or other furniture.

    (a) Pull out the most fascinating object you can find and go to the other side of the room to show it. Perhaps this is the time for all of the children to gather round to play the drum?

    (b) Go to the other side of the room and announce in a loud voice that you are going to close your eyes and take a rest, and you certainly hope that the children do not play a trick on you by sneaking out to gather in a circle around you. (When they do, acknowledge the "trick" they played on you.)

    (c) Direct the children to "find a hiding place where no one can see you" . . . then "find a spot in the middle of the room so that everyone can see you and you look very important."

(d) Beware that hiding can become a favorite game very quickly; you may well wish to have a review of the ground rules (Where is the dancing space?) if this happens more than very occasionally.

5.   Outside distractions (fire engine just went by; there is a cat fight outside; snow begins to fall, etc. . . . and everyone rushes to the window).

Don't fight it. Join the children so that it becomes a shared group experience and you can maintain the cohesiveness of the group. Then, if the event passes, return to the circle. If there is time, you can begin again . . . perhaps with a new theme suggested by the exciting event!

6.   The pervasive fantasy ("I'm not Jennifer; I'm a cat today." "Me too, . . . Meow").

When children become something or someone else, I frequently am willing to join them in the fantasy, responding to them accordingly, and then gradually working toward less restricting possibilities. (See the discussion on dealing with animal themes, page 52, Chapter 4). I do make an exception, however, when children become "Superheroes"; I insist that these characters be sent home before we dance. (Otherwise, they will return again and again.)

7.   Mass nonparticipation (usually begins when a "class leader" decides that this is an off day).

If you still have some interested children, you can continue with them. Try to build in a part for the observers ("Good, we need a wall over there; can you sit very close together so that no one can get by?") Then, after you have done a few very exciting activities, make an opportunity for the other children to reenter (perhaps the "wall" can tumble down, one piece at a time). You should not work too hard at persuading them, however, or this game (holding out against the teacher) can become a great deal of fun.

8.   Everyone copies one idea (and they suddenly seem unable to make any other response, no matter what problem is given).

Ask every child to make that same shape or motion, so that you can see what it is like when they all look the same. Allow plenty of time for a long look, making observant comments. Now direct them to make a shape that you have never seen before (or one that is not connected to the wall . . . or one that is very high—anything to break them out of the pattern). If one or two children persist, you might at first say, "Oh, I've seen that one before; I need a new one" and then ignore future repetitions.

9.   Sudden mass attack of weak kidneys (everyone has to go to the bathroom).

First check your material and your presentation; bathroomitis is frequently a function of boredom. If it is merely another case of follow the leader, you can usually put their urgency on hold by saying, in a voice full of excitement and promise, "Wait just a moment if you can, because we're about to _____ and we *really* need you." Again, do not make too big an issue of this, as it can too easily turn into a power struggle or an accident.

GENERAL INFRINGEMENTS ON ANOTHER PERSON

If children are making fun of someone else (laughing, name calling, etc.), you must stop this immediately. It is not necessary to scold the individual involved, but announce firmly and matter of factly, "In our class we don't make fun of people; we give them encouragement and help them feel good." If this problem recurs, deal with it more extensively outside the dance session, exploring with the children the feelings leading to it and resulting from it.

If the problem is generally annoying another person (feet in his or her face, etc.), the first step should be either to speak privately to the individuals involved ("In this class we stay in our own space, and do not put our feet in other people's faces."), or nonverbally separate the children involved. The second step is to do whichever of the above you have not tried. For the next step, privately say, "It looks like you don't feel like dancing today. Come sit in this chair until you can find a way to dance without disturbing others." If this is routine behavior on the part of any one child, treat it as you would disruptive behavior (see Chapter 8).

If children are actually fighting or demonstrating other aggressive behavior, your actions will have to fit the seriousness of the incident. Unless you have another adult who can remove the children involved, you will usually have to stop the session and deal with this problem as you would if it occurred in other situations. (Different schools and teachers usually have a procedure for a cooling-off time, discussion with the children, etc.)

THE FRIENDLY (OR NOT-SO-FRIENDLY) CONNECTION

Sometimes, two children will not be separated, but persist in hanging on to each other. This can easily lead to a general withdrawal from the group and, sometimes, annoying disruption. You can deal with it by structuring the next activity with directions for everyone to touch (as in a group hug) and then to touch no one.

Under most conditions, most preschoolers are not ready to really work successfully with a partner for any length of time. They ordinarily get so wrapped up playing with their friend that they lose contact with the group. Occasionally, however, a pair may actually be working very creatively and well together, even though most others in the class are not capable of partner work. Then, of course, you may want to encourage it. You may wish to size up a situation before trying to do anything about it.

Occasionally, I have had a day when a great number of the children were into pairing; then, it has become a day for working with a partner, usually with more structure than usual. (I may reassign partners, however, to make for more productive results.)

Another problem exists when everyone wants to sit next to the teacher . . . *Now.* Finding a solution to this that will seem fair to preschoolers is rare. You will spend less time in negotiation, and let them know it is not a big issue, if you suddenly find a reason for moving around or being in the middle of the circle.

LACK OF GROUP BEHAVIOR SKILLS

It sometimes surprises new teachers that one cannot give directions to preschoolers to sit in a circle or make a straight line and expect them to automatically be followed. This requires some degree of abstraction and considerable practice. (Many second graders cannot readily accomplish these tasks.) You will save yourself time and frustration if you tape a circle on the floor in the place you wish children to sit and listen or work close together. There will not be very many times you will ask preschoolers to stand in a line; when this is necessary, you will be more successful if you say "John stand here. Jane get behind John . . . etc."

Another problem under this category concerns children who cannot wait for their turn. Do not ask preschool children to spend lengthy periods of time waiting for a turn; the younger the child, the more difficult this skill. With young classes, you will want to avoid the problem by doing all the activities all together. In an older or mixed-age class, taking turns is possible; it will help to stand close to the younger, less patient children so you can touch them when necessary and give frequent reminders that everyone is special, so everyone will get a turn. It is also easier for children to wait if they are sitting rather than standing.

IT'S SUCH AN EXCITING DAY

Some days are so exciting that it may be unrealistic to compete for the children's attention and perhaps not worthwhile even to try. It is occasionally possible to have a wonderful session if you choose the exciting event(s) as the theme. To the children, dance then becomes part of the magic of the day.

Depending on the size of your group, it may seem as though it is always someone's birthday. You may choose to acknowledge this event with a special activity as part of the initial transition. Some examples are:

1. Let different body parts "say" hello and happy birthday to the honored child.

2. Use the rhythm "Happy Birthday (Jason)" to make an echo activity. (You clap the rhythm and the children clap it back.)

3. Sing "Happy Birthday to You" while the children gallop, and then freeze when they hear the birthday child's name.

EVERYONE HAS A PERSONAL STORY TO SHARE

This is fairly likely to occur after a vacation, but can happen at other times as well. (Preschoolers' stories often go on and on, and may be unrelated to the subject at hand.) The regular classroom teacher can fairly easily deal with this situation, but it can be a problem for the special teacher who is only there for a limited time period. In a small group, it is often worthwhile to spend some time listening. If you have a large group for a half-hour time slot, this may not be possible (or else there will be no time left for dance). Preschoolers can learn to defer this kind of need as they gain maturity and become less egocentric. You will need to give the children assurance that you value their thoughts and stories, and make arrangements for another time to listen. (Perhaps plan to be present while the children are on the playground.) Be prepared, though, for the children to have forgotten their urgent need by then; frequently, the need to tell a story comes more from wanting to be part of the crowd than from actually needing to share something personal and important.

Sometimes, this behavior may be a problem, not with the whole group, but with an individual who very much wants your constant attention. Gently but firmly tell the child that you cannot listen at that time, but make a date to give the child some personal attention soon. (Immediately after the class is a good time; just be sure that you fulfill whatever agreement you make.) Again, the child's need is a legitimate one, but you can help him or her learn that there are appropriate times to get the need met.

CHILDREN CANNOT "SETTLE DOWN"

Sometimes, as you attempt to begin a session, it seems that the children are too "wound up" to have the concentration dance requires. You may try your most calming voice, but the children seem to be in such high gear that they do not connect to you. This often happens after several days of bad weather (and missing outdoor play), but also may occur when children are just returning from a very energetic time outdoors and are actually tired. (Young children sometimes seem to speed up instead of slow down when they are tired!) Often, under such circumstances, teachers simply demand that the children "sit and be quiet," prescribing this as punishment as much as treatment. While this often works in taming their high spirits, a more successful approach is to work with the energy the children bring, using it and eventually channeling it. The secret of this approach is to "start where the children are," connecting to *their* energy and gradually moving to a more focused level.

One example of this approach was shown in the sample session on *snow* in Chapter 5. I remember another time that the children not only were wound up but insisted that they were frogs, too—all screaming *"Ribet!"* So, to a loud drum accompaniment, we jumped and jumped and jumped, allowing us to "connect" while they released some of their energy. Gradually, as they became fatigued, the drum beats became heavier and slower, until finally I asked all of the frogs to find a nice hole in the mud to settle into, because it was resting time for frogs. I then sang a soft song about how good it felt to relax their frog legs, arms, and heads (etc.) while I moved through the group touching them to help them relax. *Then* they were ready to begin a dance session. Whenever we can work *with* their energy rather than against it, we will usually end up happier.

THE COLLECTION OF INDIVIDUALS

Occasionally, you may have a day when, despite your best attempts to connect with the children, the group just does not come together around any focal point. The children are not being disruptive; rather, each one seems to have an individual idea that is so significant at the moment that the child is unwilling to give it up to share in any group endeavor, and you cannot find a way to tie these very different moods together. It may be rather unnerving to hear every child's strong verbal insistence on doing his or her *own* idea, but it is important not to berate the children. Rather, acknowledge them with, "Each of you seems to have your own special idea to dance in your own way. I don't think it will work for us all to dance together." Then, throw away your plan and have a time for free improvisation, with recorded music or other accompaniment; use several different types of music to fit the different styles of moving (see Chapter 7). In a small group, you may then be able to sit in a circle and have individuals share their own dances. (In a larger group, have them dance in groups; place children together who were using similar qualities so you can accompany them.) Help the children notice and appreciate the differences that make them special individuals.

ACCIDENTS

Sometimes, in almost any activity with children, toes will get stepped on or heads will get bumped. Depending on the severity of the injury, the child, and his or her mood of the day, the reaction may vary enormously, from nothing to loud wails and tears. Some children will overreact to an injury as a means of getting attention. There is always a fine line between encouraging such behavior and giving necessary and appropriate comfort to a hurt child. Your judgment at this will be better the more you know the children. If you have an assistant or another available adult, this is an enormous help; he or she can remove the child from the center of the class, determine the severity of the injury, and tend to the child's emotional and physical needs without attracting a great deal of attention. If you have to handle it yourself, you may have to stop the class briefly to evaluate the situation. It would be extremely unusual for a preschool child to get any kind of serious injury in a creative dance class. If so, of course, you must provide care immediately. For other injuries, a soothing response can be a hug coupled with a comment such as, "It really hurts when you bump your head, doesn't it? Sometimes, it helps to sit down for a couple of minutes." Also, you will probably want to double check to be sure that the other children are moving carefully and with respect for their own and others' bodies.

Toileting accidents may sometimes occur. If you teach young preschoolers, you are probably used to dealing with this situation with as little attention as possible and encouraging the children to handle clean-up themselves as much as they can, to encourage responsibility. However, wet spots on the floor can be slippery and, therefore, dangerous for dance. If such problems occur regularly in your classroom, have cleaning supplies at hand so you can casually mop up while maintaining the continuity of the class.

This, of course, does not exhaust the list of "everything children can possibly do to make teaching more difficult." Hopefully, however, it will get you through the initial obstacles in trying a new activity, and give you courage to meet the challenges that children present.

CHAPTER 7

Sources and Stimuli—
The Integrated Curriculum

In most school situations beyond preschool, much of the child's learning is fragmented as he or she proceeds from math class to language arts to physical education. For the preschool child (and probably naturally for all of us), learning is a much more integrated experience. Is it art or science as a child mixes colors and discovers that blue and yellow make green? The child notices curves and angles in letters and then makes them with his or her own body or draws them in the air; is this language arts or dance?

Everything in the young child's world forms the preschool curriculum, and most ideas and objects in the world can provide more than one category of experience. The idea of an integrated curriculum is not to use one medium (such as dance) to teach another, but to allow and encourage children to use all of their senses to experience the world through a multitude of viewpoints. For example, when we use *snow* as a theme for a class, we are not trying to teach children about snow through movement. Rather, just as we want children to know snow by seeing it, we also want them to use their kinesthetic sense to experience the designs, patterns, and qualities.

The sources and stimuli for dance are all around us, in everything with shape or motion. The natural world is an obvious choice, as we observe the weather, the seasons, growing things, wind, water, fire. The manmade or technological world may seem further removed, but all sorts of machines, vehicles, construction equipment, clocks, etc., can be exciting to deal with in dance. The holidays, with particular festive shapes, activities, legends, and feelings, are a frequent resource for classes. Even very common everyday activities and events can be experienced in new ways by abstracting the motion and going beyond pantomime—bread baking as shown in Chapter 4, with its rising, punching, and shaping; clothes washing, with churning, suspending points from a clothesline, stiffening with starch, wrinkling, and flattening. Ordinary objects can be manipulated in many ways—cardboard boxes, crepe paper streamers, sheets of tissue paper, and so forth. In the Appendix, there is a listing of some ideas from the world around us that have led to exciting classes with preschoolers; you will undoubtedly think of many more. These ideas may be developed into a lesson as described in Chapter 4. Ideas from specific curricular areas are discussed below.

MUSIC[1]

Other art forms seem naturally related to dance. One of the first sources that comes to mind is music. We have already discussed the desirability of

---

[1]See Appendix A for additional suggestions on selecting and using music for preschool dance.

creating your own songs and sounds with instruments and (especially) your own voice. In small-sized groups, children, too, can be encouraged to create their own sounds to accompany their own dances (and, as they get older, those of other children). Children can also listen to different sounds and translate these into motion. (Is it a strong sound or a light one? Is it a high or a low sound? Does it last a long time or a short time?)

Teaching Idea: Responding to Different Instrumental Sounds

Concept: Basic Actions

Activities:

(a) Select three instruments with distinctive sounds (such as maracas, cymbal, clavs).

(b) Play each instrument one at a time and explore what kind of movement fits the sound (such as shaking, sustained stretching, tiptoeing). The movement of each child need not be the same, but the quality should be representative of the sound for the child.

(c) Dance structure: Alternate playing each of the instruments, letting children identify the sound for each section and respond with appropriate movement.

Teaching Note: Notice the different responses made by different children to the same sound. Support individual responses by giving feedback such as, "Jason is shaking his fingers. Melissa is shaking her whole self."

Records of instrumental music can be helpful as accompaniment by providing a sense of ongoingness and group cohesiveness, setting a mood (especially the important magical quality), and stimulating particular qualities in movement. (Bouncy music will almost always produce bouncy movement, so be aware of this kind of effect as you select music.)

What about just putting on some music for free improvisation, asking children to "dance whatever you feel like?" A basic rhythmic response occurs spontaneously as early as a few months of age. For many individuals, such open release and self-expression through movement continue to be comfortable and satisfying as long as the setting is one of psychological safety. Even by preschool age, however, some children will feel very self-conscious about sharing themselves in this way.

Ideally, your role in this situation consists of more than selecting music with a regular beat and a good sense of motion, and then turning on the phonograph. Some children will respond immediately and openly to the music; they will usually have little awareness of what they are doing, however, and may repeat the same movement over and over again, seemingly "stuck" in one pattern. You can encourage greater awareness and extension of their movement vocabulary by using the techniques for reinforcing awareness discussed in Chapter 5. What about children who, at first glance, seem unresponsive—children who are "just sitting (or standing) there?" If you look more closely you will be able to find some movement, some participation, even though they may not be aware of it—a nodding of the head, a bouncing of the knees, scratching a foot. These responses should be noted with enthusiasm equal to that given to the more active children, so they will know they are valued members of the group and that their responses are acceptable. As these children feel safer, they eventually will begin to use larger body movement as well.

As you respond verbally to the movement of different children, you will want to "try it on" yourself—to enjoy and/or expand it. For example, if you take on a child's pattern of forward and backward arm swings, you can extend it perhaps by reaching up to the ceiling each time, finding new directions for the swing, or letting the whole body become involved, maybe even taking you into a turn . . . verbalizing in a few words what you are doing. The child (as well as, perhaps, other children) may copy your movement or (hopefully) begin to feel enough confidence and sense of adventure to try his or her own variation.

The more you enjoy this kind of improvisation, the more comfortable your children are likely to feel. If you do feel uncomfortable, it usually is better to acknowledge your feelings to the children ("I sometimes feel a little embarrassed when I dance just the way I feel. I wish I didn't.") rather than just acting embarrassed.

The length of time that different children can "stay with" free improvisation varies enormously. At the moment you are realizing some children have lost interest, other children may be heartbroken to stop this very personal kind of expression. You will find it very helpful to have alternative activities set up for those who have lost interest, so that children who desire to continue may do so.

Another use for instrumental music involves a more "planned" response. With the children, you can listen to the music, identifying major characteristics and changes (slow parts and fast parts) and discussing how to show, for example, strong, loud parts of the music as they dance. You may experience the same piece of music over and over again on different days, and the children's awareness will deepen as they begin to hear more in the music and respond to it more fully. Be sure, however, that you begin with fairly short pieces that are clear and simple (not too many changes), and limit your discussion to only a couple of points during one session.

Teaching Idea: Creating a Dance to Recorded Music ("In the Hall of the Mountain King")

Concepts: Basic Actions, Range (will vary according to music selected)

Activities:

(a) Explore small movement (tiptoe or blink the eyes, for example), large movement (jump), and medium-sized movement (pump arms).

(b) Play a recording of "In the Hall of the Mountain King." Ask the children to listen for the small quiet sounds, big loud sounds, and in between sounds. Note that the change is gradual.

(c) Dance structure: Play the recording again, asking the children to dance small movement when the music sounds small and quiet, large movement when the music sounds big and loud, and medium-sized movement when the music sounds in between.

Teaching Note: Even as children are just listening to the music for the first time, they will begin to move, for children listen with their whole bodies. Encourage movement they can do while sitting to help them feel the different qualities.

Some recordings of vocal music can be used similarly to ones without words, when the words are nondirective or less important than the total mood. There are also many records of vocal music produced especially for "children's dance." While some of these are more open-ended than others, most are directions for action songs. This kind of record can serve many purposes. The activity is usually a great deal of fun for children, just as most motor activity is fun, and they derive a lot of pleasure from doing something "right" (being at the right place at the right time). The children can also learn some body concepts through these activities. In addition, such records can be helpful in conserving the teacher's energy; all of the planning is done and the voice on the record can practically take over for the teacher. As helpful as such records may be, however, they do not take the place of the kind of creative dance experiences discussed in this book, any more than coloring in coloring books (also a pleasant and sometimes useful activity for children) takes the place of free drawing and painting. Sometimes, these records can be used as a jumping-off point for more creative experiences in dance.

Teaching Idea: Dance to a Song (tune of "Here Comes Peter Cottontail")

Concepts: Basic Actions, Shapes

Activities:

(a) Explore jumping with different variations.

(b) Explore making individual body shapes.

(c) Sing: Here come all my *jumping* friends
           Jumping just to make a dance,
           Jumping, jumping—magic's on the way.
           Filling up the dancing space
           With everybody's special *shape* (pause)
  (softer) Feel the magic that we have today.

(d) Dance structure:
   - Repeat the first three lines of the song while the children jump.
   - Repeat the next three lines of the song. As the children hear the word *shape*, each child freezes in his or her own shape. Hold the freeze until hearing what kind of movement comes next.
   - Repeat the song, using *wiggling* instead of *jumping*. Repeat the song using other movement words.

Teaching Note:
   - Encourage children to offer suggestions of other kinds of movement—"What kind of a dance should it be next?"
   - In addition to basic actions, use other elements to make a backwards dance, a slow-motion dance, etc. (see Chapter 2).

Various action songs and finger plays that you sing with children fall into the same category. Most preschoolers love mastering these skills and, at certain ages, may even become adamant about the correct way to perform them. You can encourage the children to create new motions or new verses to these songs. (What other body part could you use for the hammer? How else could we show the rain falling? Where else could the bumblebee fly?) Other songs that you know can also be adapted for dance sessions; for example, "Here Comes Peter Cottontail" can stimulate a variety of locomotor movements if "hopping" is changed to a different kind of motion in each verse.

LITERATURE

Another art form with much to offer as source material for dance is literature. Much poetry for young children is rich with images that can be used to set a general mood, or the words may develop a rhythm pattern. Some poems may be danced to line by line, like an action song. Any books of children's poetry will offer you many ideas; a few suggestions are given in Appendix C.

Children may also create poetry in response to dance activities. In a class one spring, for example, we explored movement the children noticed in the spring. Some of the suggestions included clouds (making soft cloud shapes), pansies (making shapes, moving in the wind), new grass (popping up), trees (blowing in the wind), rain (lightly falling), and eggs hatching (popping out). I then solicited images for a poem, providing the form but not the words, which came from these 3- to 5-year-old children:

> Crack! Crack!
> When the clouds get mad they hit together and the rain goes
> pitter patter
> And grass and flowers start popping up
> And trees blow in the wind.
> The birds come back and they find a place in a perfect pine,
> And the baby birds pop out of their eggs
> Crack! Crack! Crack!

Children's books, too, can be used in very exciting ways. There are a number of books written about dance and dancers that can give children a glimpse of the larger world of dance; these books can also set a mood for dance. There are others that seem even better designed for this purpose; while they don't usually specify many particular movements, they give a real sense of the magical quality of dance and sometimes can stimulate a very exciting session (see the book list in Appendix C).

Some children's books can be used even more directly in a dance session, with the book itself actually serving as the unifying theme. Since preschool children are accustomed to being read to, this can be a good way to begin doing some dance activities, turning occasional points of the

---

Teaching Idea: Dance to a Poem ("Mrs. Peck-Pigeon")

Concept: Basic Actions (will vary according to poem selected)

Activities:

   (a)   Read the poem "Mrs. Peck-Pigeon"[2]

> Mrs. Peck-Pigeon
> Is picking for bread,
> Bob-bob-bob
> Goes her little round head.
> Tame as a pussy-cat
> In the street,
> Step-step-step
> Go her little red feet.
> With her little red feet
> And her little round head,
> Mrs. Peck-Pigeon
> Goes picking for bread.
>   *Eleanor Farjeon*

   (b)   Explore the movement words—picking, bobbing, stepping.

   (c)   Ask the children for suggestions of other small movements. Explore these.

   (d)   Dance structure: Reread the poem while the children dance using picking, bobbing, stepping, and/or other small movements.

Teaching Note: During exploration, some children may tire of small movement and begin to use large movement as contrast. Be ready to respond in a positive way—perhaps improvise about "Mrs. Gigantic goes jumping for bread." Then perform both dances to give the children a chance to use both kinds of movement.

---

book into kinesthetic as well as listening experiences. With some books, the imagery on practically every page can be developed and used as a jumping-off point for dance activities. The children will not be "acting out" the story, but rather exploring in movement terms many of the images present. The structure provided by a book can be especially helpful for a teacher less experienced in leading dance; many potentially difficult

---

[2]Farjeon, Eleanor. *Eleanor Farjeon's Poems for Children.* Philadelphia: J. B. Lippincott, 1951.

moments can be handled with a return to the circle or cluster to "see what happens on the next page of the book."

Selecting a book for this purpose involves different criteria than just picking a good story for listening, or even for dramatization. Look for books with vivid movement imagery—action words or ideas that can easily be translated into movement terms. If the actions are primarily everyday activities, you will need to think of ways to expand them beyond pantomime. The images and qualities in the book should generally be more significant than the characters or the plot, since no one child will be "playing" any character and you will want to be able to explore ideas fully, without the children being too anxious to find out what happens next. If you think you have a good choice except for a too-exciting plot, make sure that the children are very familiar with the story before you begin; otherwise, they will be so anxious to hear the story that they will have little interest in dancing!

Some books may have only an occasional image worth exploring in movement; these provide primarily listening experiences, with just moments of dance time. If you are really choosing a book as the theme for the class, however, it is helpful to have a book without too many words—just a line or two per page, and no more than one or two movements on each. If an otherwise good selection is too wordy for use, you will need to paraphrase the story in order to maintain the continuity of the dance session.

Do not be too concerned about the length of the book, as long as it can be dealt with in one- or two-page units; you may wish to spend many sessions on a single book. In using a book in this way, you will essentially be working page by page, translating each into a movement concept and then into activities.

You may well find that, by using books as source material for dance, your children will get their own ideas for dancing, even from books that you have not intended to be dance experiences!

Teaching Idea: Using a Book as a Theme for a Dance Session (*Swimmy,* by L. Leonni)

Activities:

(a) Select an idea from each page, translate it into a movement concept and develop it through exploring and then structuring it into a *dance*.

(b) Example from the first page:
Idea—Swimmy swam faster than his brothers and sisters.
Concept—Speed
Activities
- Perform a simple movement, such as clapping, and ask the children to perform the same movement faster, then slower.
- Repeat with other movements. Select individual children to serve as leaders for the same process.

(c) Example from the second page:
Idea—Darting through the waves
Concept—Darting (sudden movement in a direct line)
Activities
- Demonstrate a darting movement with a chosen body part.
- Ask the children if the movement looked slow or fast, wiggly or straight.
- Explore darting movement with body parts and the whole body (running).
- Dance Structure: Dart one part, then another part; then, dart the whole body through space and freeze. Repeat several times.

DRAMA

If you already do creative drama in your classroom, you are aware that, while drama deals with more realistic and everyday movement, there are many areas in which the two art forms overlap and support each other. The sensory awareness activities done in creative drama to increase perception and sensory recall can be of benefit in dance as well. They increase children's readiness to sense movement and support the magical quality that is so essential for dance to happen. Listening, looking, tasting, smelling, and touching may often serve as transitions to a dance session or be part of it.

As noted throughout this book, pantomime is not the same as dance. However, if your goal is to develop skill in pantomime, it can be made clearer through the understanding of movement elements: What direction and pathway does your hand move when opening a door? What parts of your body might you use to push a heavy box across the floor? Do you need a strong or a light touch to pick a caterpillar off a plant? Dramatic imagery may also be used with basic movement, leading to action pantomimes: How would you walk if you were walking on eggs? Through molasses? On slippery stones across a stream?

Noticing and expressing feelings is important, not only in drama, but in other arts as well as in everyday life; sometimes, it is difficult for preschoolers to move beyond very superficial expressions of feeling in drama activities. Again, the elements of movement can provide a vocabulary leading to awareness of internal states and their outward expression: Does *sad* feel heavy or light? Does it feel curved or straight? Slow or fast? These sorts of questions could lead to a "dance about sadness" or a dramatization of sadness. In any case, they will help take children to an awareness of sadness that goes beyond just a turned-down mouth.

VISUAL ARTS

The motivation for drawing and painting comes from two sources—the kinesthetic sense (the feeling of and pleasure in the action itself) and the desire to make a form that one sees.[3] The kinesthetic sense motivates the child's early scribbles, as well as much of the "doodling" adults do. Many famous works of art, especially some "modern art," are as concerned with what something feels like as with what it looks like. Awakening the kinesthetic sense, developing an inside awareness of motion and feelings, can stimulate this kind of artistic expression. Especially if done right after a dance session, children may express their sensations from the class in drawing and painting: strength and lightness; tension and relaxation; movements such as vibrating, swinging, and falling. Large sheets of paper are most helpful so that children can maintain some of the same sensations while drawing that they felt while moving.

---

[3]For an excellent discussion of the relationship between these two art forms, see *Towards Dance and Art* by Elizabeth Watts (London: Lepus Books, 1977.)

Teaching Idea: Draw a Dance

Concept: Basic Action

Activities:

(a) Explore any movement (such as shaking). Use large parts and small ones; use different speeds and degrees of tension.

(b) Make a "shaking dance."

(c) Distribute art materials for children to draw a "shaking dance."(Each child may draw his or her own, or the drawing can be a collective effort.)

Teaching Note: Ask the children to remember inside what a shake feels like before they begin to draw. Describe their responses: "This looks like a slow, heavy, wiggle; this one looks strong and fast."

Teaching Idea: Dance a Picture

Concept: Air Pattern

Activities:

(a) Present a simple design to the children.

(b) Explore the design or design quality (such as circularity) in movement, using individual body parts as well as the whole body.

(c) The dance structure will be based on the design. Children may select a starting and ending shape that is like the design.

Teaching Note: Some pictures present a feeling or quality more than a design. This also can be translated into movement terms.

A dance session can also stimulate art work concerned with reproducing visual form—making what you see. While preschool children are not concerned with accurate reproduction, dance provides experiences that are related to this skill. Through dance, children increase their perception of the form of the human body at rest and in motion (Where does the body bend? How high can the arms reach?) as well as other objects that may be dealt with in a class. They become aware of positive and negative space, the difference between curved and straight lines, and distances and relationships. They *see* more. Many themes explored in dance have a natural extension in art (and vice versa). For example, a class that explores the shapes and pathways of falling leaves might be followed by making a collage of gathered leaves.

SCIENCE, LANGUAGE ARTS, MATH, AND SOCIAL STUDIES

Other more "academic" subject matter is also interrelated with dance. Again, the idea is not so much to teach math through movement, but to provide opportunities to experience concepts in different ways. Many movement concepts are also part of the science curriculum, particularly the elements of energy and time. Many times, children's observations of the natural world can be ideas for dance—the way the sand flows, the shapes of ice crystals, the floating of a leaf on the water. These ideas can be developed into entire sessions, as was demonstrated with the theme of *snow* in Chapter 4. In addition, briefer movement activities may be incorporated into a science lesson. For example, as children explore magnets, they can also explore what it would feel like if their feet were pulled together like magnets, or if they tried to walk when a very strong magnet was pulling their feet to the floor. In a science lesson, "doing it with the body" can make an idea easier to understand and harder to forget.

For language arts, communication skills in general are the core of the curriculum for young children, and nonverbal communication skills are as important in human interaction as verbal ones. Dance is a way of speaking with the body, and children gain practice in the use of symbols, the basis of all language.

Communication skills in general improve as children develop more awareness of their own feelings and those of others and widen their range of expression. More specific language arts skills that are part of dance class include developing and remembering sequences (such as run-turn-sink-roll) and building vocabulary. (Children can "own" new words once they experience them.) Perception and reproduction of visual patterns, basic skills for reading and writing, are also experienced in dance through activities with air and floor patterns. Sound discrimination is part of both subjects as well; in dance sessions, activities can be planned for children to respond differently to different sounds (make a hard shape when you hear the sound of hard *c* and a soft shape when you hear the sound of soft *c*). Stories and poems, as previously discussed in this section, also provide exciting experiences in dance.

Teaching Idea: Gesture Dance

Concepts: Body Parts; Basic Actions

Activities:

    (a)   Explore an everyday gesture, such as a wave good-bye. Change it: make it larger or smaller, faster or slower. Use other body parts.

    (b)   Try it with other gestures, such as those meaning "come on," "stop," or "I don't know."

    (c)   Dance structure: Make a dance in three parts, using one gesture as the basis for each part.

Teaching Note: In singing an accompaniment for the dance, include cues reminding children of some of the variations they explored earlier. Otherwise, they may tend to return to the everyday form.

Mathematics is basically the study of quantitative relationships; so, dance activities concerned with relationships of time (as in rhythm) and space (size relationships) are supportive of math. Appropriate movement experiences can help children understand the meaning of *more than* and *less than, faster* and *slower,* and *larger* and *smaller.* Activities involving remembering sequences and patterns (what to do where) are also extremely significant for the development of higher-level math skills.

The social studies curriculum also contains areas that are part of dance. A child's sense of self in space is essential to the development of map skills. Also, many kinds of work movement can be abstracted to become sources for dance experiences.

Even more significant in the social studies curriculum for preschoolers are such basic concepts as sharing, cooperation, and respect for differences. While such concerns should be primary during every session, and will be acknowledged informally, it is also possible to deal with them as ideas for dance. For example, children can explore dancing close together, discovering that they must use small movements to keep from bumping each other. Individual children can lead the group at times, for experiences in leading and following. A dance can be made that celebrates individual differences in doing any movement, using a dance structure involving three parts: John's way, Karen's way, and Michael's way.

Teaching Idea: Workshop Dance

Concept: Basic Actions (with variations)

Activities:

(a) Select several common tools, such as a hammer, saw, and screwdriver.

(b) Pantomime using each tool, then explore the movement by doing it with other body parts or by changing the speed, level, direction, etc.

(c) Dance structure: Make a dance in three parts: hammering, sawing, and turning.

Teaching Note: Whatever kind of work activity is used should be familiar to the children before they begin to change it.

Teaching Idea: Taking Turns

Concepts: Basic Actions; Freezing

Activities:

(a) Explore several basic actions, in alternation with a total freeze. Add music, giving the children a free choice of movement, in alternation with a freeze.

(b) Dance structure: Begin in a freeze while the children dance. Then, the children freeze while you dance. Repeat several times.

Accompaniment: Recorded music

Teaching Note: The same dance can be done in pairs, with children taking turns with a partner. This is only possible if children are able to work successfully with a partner.

Teaching Idea: Sharing Space

Concept: Positive and Negative Space

Activities:

(a) Explore making shapes with "holes." Be sure the children are seeing the empty spaces in their shapes.

(b) Explore traveling through space and then freezing (on signal) in a shape with holes.

(c) Dance structure: Assign each child a partner. One child makes a shape and freezes. The child's partner then makes a shape that uses some of the first child's empty space and freezes. The first child then travels to a new spot in the room and freezes. The second child joins his or her partner and makes a shape that fills an empty space. Continue. (Demonstrate the idea to make it clear.)

Accompaniment: Improvised song

Teaching Note: This activity is only for children who have the maturity to work with a partner, or in a parent-child class. It will help to pair children according to obvious characteristics, such as age or gender. That way you can cue them in your song, such as, "Girls travel to a new place, find a shape that has some holes, and freeze."

VIEWING PERFORMANCES

One further area should be mentioned in discussing the preschool curriculum: viewing performances of dance (and other art forms) that are designed for audiences of young children. Such performances, if designed and carried out by people who know both dance and children, can give a child a better sense of the magical quality than many years of talking about it, as well as a real *AHA* moment: "So this is what it means to be a dancer!" They can add an excitement to future dance sessions that is impossible to capture in any other way. Many performances, if done in a lecture-demonstration style, can also help children become a more perceptive audience by pointing out elements to watch for. ("Notice in the next dance how the dancers use different parts of their bodies like imaginary paintbrushes, to make designs in the air.") They can also be the source for many dance experiences to follow, with children creating their own versions of dances they have observed.

Unfortunately, such performances, while increasing in number, are still a rarity in most parts of the country and, of course, the quality varies. It would be worth making a longer field trip than you would ordinarily consider with preschoolers to have a chance to view a good one. If a professional dance company visits your town as part of the National Endowment for the Arts Dance Touring Program, they may offer a children's performance. The most likely sources are local professional or amateur dance companies (mostly located in larger cities) or colleges or universities with dance programs. Call the director to indicate your interest and see if the company would consider doing such a performance; most preschools are so anxious for their children to have this kind of experience that all seats are likely to be sold out well ahead of time. If they have never done one, you might even offer your resources to a group of students who know dance but not preschoolers, to help them create a program appropriate for this age group—one that does not "talk down" to children, but uses simple and clear presentation. The value of this kind of experience makes it worth a great deal of effort.

CHAPTER 8

Children with Special Needs

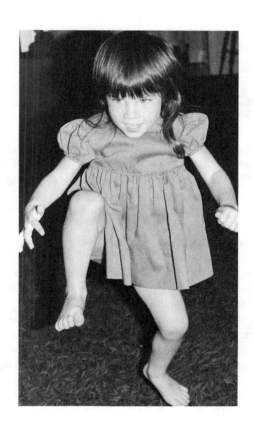

All children need to move and to experience what is magical and wonderful about themselves and their world. Dance is one important way for all children to satisfy this need. However, many of the activities described in this book are not accessible to all children, particularly those with sensory or orthopedic disabilities, children who do not understand verbal language, or those who do not have the social skills to work in a group. Dance can still be a part of these children's lives, although it requires some adaptation. In reality, all classes require adaptation to fit the needs of the particular children involved. Because of this, teaching dance to children classified as having special needs does not feel much different for me than working with children considered to be "normal."

This chapter offers suggestions for making dance accessible to children with selected special needs. It is not intended to be an introduction to special education. If you are a special education teacher, you already know (and need to know) a great deal more about teaching these children. If you are a preschool teacher with an occasional special child in your class, you will need to consult with specialists and the child's parents regarding how to best meet the child's needs throughout the school day. Additional resources on dance for special populations are included in the Appendix.

VERY YOUNG CHILDREN (CHRONOLOGICALLY AND/OR DEVELOPMENTALLY UNDER AGE 3)

Many very young children are preverbal. Even those who understand a great deal of spoken language may speak little themselves. They deal mostly in the concrete reality of the present as it appears to them. Their body control is much less than that of older children. They ordinarily have little sense of being part of a group, and may not even respond to directions given generally to a whole group (particularly if they have not previously had group experience). Interaction with these children is usually on a one-to-one basis even though there may be several children in a room. However, just because very young children are more limited in their experiences does not mean that they do not think and feel, or that they cannot participate in dance.

With very young children, you should build into your day activities that we may term "predance" or even dance "readiness"—activities that lead to, support, and reinforce an understanding of dance. There are three categories of these predance experiences. The first is the encouragement of movement in general. This includes providing an environment where movement can happen, including empty space and interesting apparatus. Preferably, there should be an environment for movement both indoors and out. Encouraging movement also involves giving approval to children when they move, letting them know that you value their effort and exploration, regardless of their skill level. We need to give our attentiveness and enthusiasm to children involved in gross motor play and let them see us as adults experiencing pleasure in using our own bodies. (We need to move and play *with* them at times, and not only sit and watch them.)

The second category involves encouragement of creative activity in general. Children should have many opportunities to explore, to make choices, to do things their own way, and to know that adults value their contributions. This implies providing an environment in which there are many possibilities for diversity, many materials that have open-ended uses (e.g., toys and other items that can be played with in many different ways).

The third category involves encouragement of sensory awareness. This includes providing an environment in which there are interesting things to touch, taste, smell, hear, and see. Beyond that, it involves calling attention to special experiences—the cool feel of a piece of satin, the clear sound of a silver bell, the fragile wonder of the robin's egg. This lets children know that such moments are significant enough that you, as an adult, will take the time to savor them.

Dance with very young children may easily flow out of the kinds of activities indicated previously. This will occur in spontaneous movements more than in planned sessions, and you may feel more like a follower than a leader. Your major job will be to connect to what each child is doing and expand his or her awareness of it. For example, you may see a child swaying from side to side (or wrinkling his nose or wiggling her toes—or whatever!). You will notice not only that the child is moving, but also something particular about the movement (the action, the body part, or some other aspect), and then respond to the child. Some ways you might respond are:

1.   Copying the child's action (wiggling *your* toes).

2.   Varying the child's action (wiggling your fingers or bending and straightening your toes).

3.   Simply doing your own dance close by the child (comparable to "parallel play" among young children).

4.   Naming the child's movement ("You're wiggling your toes!" or improvising a song about Keisha wiggling her toes).

Whatever response you make will have two effects: it will let the child know you *like* his or her movement and it will help the child *notice* his or her own movement. (The child may not even be aware of the movement until your response.)

As I interact with very young children, they may copy my movement, but I am generally more interested in having them enjoy and become aware of their own movement. When I dance with a child, I do it for the pleasure of sharing the experience rather than getting the child to move as I do. I have found, however, that when I am actively involved (rather than just sitting and watching), most children will continue dancing for a longer period and will request the activity more often. (We must remember, though, that children have their own sense of time, and we need to respect their decision to stop, whenever it comes.)

Just as with older children, some sort of accompaniment will often sustain the very young child's attention to movement (especially if you freeze when the music ends and begin to dance when the music begins again). Playing music for a shared dance time and *responding* to a child as suggested above is one of the best ways to encourage a very young child to dance. Each of the children can continue to move in his or her own way while you respond to individuals one at a time.

There are also times when an adult may initiate dance or dance-like activities with very young children. This is particularly appropriate with children who do not initiate themselves. Our first task is to get their attention. This means saying the child's name and getting close to the child so that you can be seen and heard. In the case of children with severe developmental delays, it is often helpful to initiate attention the same way each time; for example, you might say, "Anna, look at me!"

It is often appropriate to pick up a small child so he or she can experience dance while being held. Most parents do this naturally with their babies, singing and/or dancing to music. Occasionally, adults may get too rough or frighten a child, which should be avoided. If a developmentally delayed child is too heavy for an adult to lift, yet this kind of physical contact is desired, the adult can sit or kneel on the floor to hold the child and still sway or rock to music.

Whenever we attempt to communicate with someone who does not understand us, even someone who speaks a different language, it is helpful to use other signals in addition to the words. Multisensory cues are particularly important in helping very young children understand us. For example, if you are trying to help children move with a *floppy* quality, say the word and demonstrate the movement at the same time. Other signals include using music that clearly reflects this quality, or demonstrating with a rag doll. In the case of children with verbal communication difficulties, you may also use sign language to say *floppy*.

Repetition is important to all young children; in fact, adults often tire of a favorite activity or story before children do! Repeating activities in successive lessons is particularly important for very young children, both in giving a sense of security and in facilitating learning.

When young children have severe and profound mental handicaps, it may seem that the major task of education should be to work on functional activities, and that such children could not "appreciate" dance anyway, much less be able to dance themselves. However, even these children can appreciate the motion and touch of a caring adult who dances while holding them, and most will give a motor response to music with a strong beat. While these activities may seem less significant than learning to sit up, the experience of dance is a special aspect of humanness that should not be ignored. Appropriate dance experiences, however limited they might be, are part of acknowledging the humanity of these special children.

CHILDREN WITH ORTHOPEDIC DISABILITIES

All children, and adults, need to like their bodies in order to like themselves. Helping the child to like his or her body is probably the greatest contribution dance can make to the child with an orthopedic disability. Rehabilitative training, which is very necessary, works primarily on what the child cannot do, whereas preschool dance works a great deal with what the child can already do. While some exercises may be woven into the class and/or used in an introduction, a more important reason for these children to dance is to experience joy and success with their bodies.

If children do not have use of one part of their body, they can dance with other parts. Many dance activities can be experienced by those who are nonlocomotor, even those who can move only the upper body. Props may be especially useful for these children in order to extend what the body can do. Sticks with balloons attached, scarves, crepe paper strips, and the like are popular for use in this way. (It is, of course, important that children stay far enough apart so they will not injure each other.) If the child has a prosthesis, encourage its use as a body part, which it is.

Orthopedically disabled preschoolers may be mainstreamed into a class with other children. In this case, it is especially important to know ahead of time as much as possible about the strengths and weaknesses of these children. I also find it helpful to speak to the mainstreamed child before we start, to let the child know I may need help in understanding what he or she can do. It helps both of us if I can say, "Mark, can you do this?" as comfortably as I would ask any other child if he or she could reach a toy on a shelf. I try to plan activities that all children can do. However, sometimes the larger group may need to do some activity beyond the limits of the mainstreamed child. In such cases, I try to offer an alternative to any child who cannot participate in the usual way, even if it is only to "watch to see if they *really* freeze." As children begin to feel more comfortable with their bodies and with me, they make their own adaptations and suggestions ("I'll shake when they run "). Sometimes, neither of us can think of a solution; in those cases, it is better to admit that we are stumped than for me to get too embarrassed to say anything.

Whenever I have had an orthopedically disabled student of any age, it has helped the rest of us find new possibilities we might not have found otherwise. For example, I used to use wiggling the fingers and toes when children needed to focus their energy by moving a small body part. It took a child without fingers to help me realize that eyes and tongues can also dance.

CHILDREN WITH SEVERE VISUAL AND HEARING LOSSES

At the preschool age, most of these children are likely to be enrolled in special education facilities rather than mainstreamed, so they receive intensive help in developing communication skills. Movement of some kind is ordinarily a part of these programs; however, these children may not be given as many opportunities for creative and expressive activities as are other children. Sometimes, arts specialists may be brought in to provide special activities; this has been my role in working with these children.

In leading dance experiences for hearing impaired preschool children, the biggest challenge is communication. Knowing sign language is extremely helpful; otherwise, you must have an interpreter in order to be successful. Without someone to sign, it is very difficult to get preschool children to do anything other than imitate you. If you use an interpreter, you must stand near each other so that the children can see both of you. Even when children can see both of you, they will not be able to concentrate on watching both at the same time, so it is usually better to work sequentially: first you speak and demonstrate, and then let the interpreter communicate; then, if necessary, demonstrate again. The dance teacher should speak clearly, using as few words as possible, in order to have the class flow without long stops.

Even if you do know sign, you will find challenges in leading dance sessions. For example, the sign to *freeze*, involving gripped fingers, is so graphic that the children's first tendency is to freeze in that shape every time! It is often helpful to give the directions in sign and then demonstrate at least two different ways to help the children find other shapes for freezing.

When you and an interpreter are communicating with the children, it is important that they be able to see you. It is usually no problem to have all the children face you when they are moving in place, but it is too limiting for children to have to always face one direction while moving through space. It helps to give all necessary directions *before* students start to travel and have a signal that is visible anywhere in the room (I use a single flash of the lights) that means "freeze and face the teacher." It is also useful to have an established place students go to receive more detailed directions. I use a taped semicircle for hearing impaired children, instead of a full circle as I use with other children, so that all the children can see me from the front. Choose your location with regard to light, avoiding glare.

Teachers of hearing impaired children know that it is important to use all of the hearing children do have. This means using accompaniment in class. The vibrations of a large hand drum can be perceived by many deaf children. Recorded music is more likely to be heard (or felt) if the speaker is placed on the floor, especially if the floor is wooden. Place the microphones used with the children's auditory equipment in front of the speaker, but use normal volume. I try to use music with both high-pitched and low tones to take advantage of the hearing abilities of different children.

With these modifications to facilitate communication, hearing impaired children can be just as successful in dance as their hearing counterparts.

Young children who are blind or partially sighted present an even greater challenge in dance. All of us who have donned a blindfold know that absence of vision produces anxiety that makes us move tentatively. Free running, jumping, and the like are usually not part of the movement repertoire of these children, which hinders their motor development. Most blind preschoolers move more like younger children, so the suggestions given for very young children also apply here.

First of all, you need to make an environment in which it is safe for the children to move. Depending on the amount of sight the children possess, this may mean dancing with them only one at a time or in a small group with one adult per child.

Since some rhythmic response to music is natural to all of us who can hear it, this can be a good starting place for visually impaired children. You may start with music with such a strong beat that it is hard *not* to move; then, gradually include other kinds of music as well. If children do respond with some kind of movement (such as bouncing), you can begin with that movement, helping children to extend the movement and try other possibilities. It is important to name the movement you see the child do to help build a vocabulary for communication about movement.

At some point, a sense of touch is important to expand what the child hears. You may, for example, ask the child to touch your toes to feel them dancing, or you may touch the child's toes with a bouncing hand. You can also pick the child up and dance with him or her to the music. This allows the child to have some sensory experiences in movement (such as feeling a breeze against the skin while twirling) that are not yet possible for the child moving alone. It also helps build trust and confidence in you, if you do not do movement for which the child is not yet ready. As you dance with the child, use verbal language that names the movement you are doing.

Once the child gains trust in you, he or she will be more willing to move freely while holding your hand or hands. Then, ask the child to move to you (to your voice), first when you stay in the same place each time, and then when you move to a different place in the room. At first, this may involve a couple of tentative steps but, eventually, both the distance and the movement repertoire may be expanded.

You should also use music and touching to help communicate concepts. For example, children need to touch your shape (all over, so they can get a sense of the whole body involvement) to understand this concept. Feeling different curved shapes made out of different materials is important in helping them understand curves. Hearing light, gentle music and feeling a feather against the skin can help build an understanding of lightness that can be transferred into their movement.

Children with less severe visual losses may be able to participate in a group dance experience if they are close enough to the teacher to see what he or she is doing. For partially sighted children, dance may be an activity in which they do not perceive themselves as handicapped.

CHILDREN WHO ARE PERSISTENTLY DISRUPTIVE

It would be unusual to have a preschool class without one or two children who are often "out of bounds." These children have a high need for physical activity and may have trouble focusing. They seem to "zoom" rather than walk from one place to another. For these children, finding the "quiet place inside" may at first seem an impossibility, and they may get in the way of other children finding *their* magic. These children may not intend to disrupt the class, but they often do. Some of them may be diagnosed hyperactive, although most are just at the upper end of the normal range. A surprising number of disruptive children end up being less difficult in dance class than at other times, as long as

- Their quiet selves, however small, are carefully nurtured.

- They are allowed to use the intensity with which they routinely approach the world.

- The activity is carefully structured.

Most of the following suggestions are valuable for most children, but essential for active and disruptive children.

Children who are easily overstimulated need as much help as possible in finding the quiet part of themselves. Try to remove distracting things from the environment while dancing. (For example, move the gerbils so they cannot be seen!) Give plenty of time for transition from activities such as playground time that you know make all children "wilder." Teach the children how to relax (see Chapter 2). It may take very active children longer to relax; you may leave them lying on the floor the longest in a relaxation activity, giving them the time they need.

Whenever these children find the soft, quiet part of themselves, be sure to acknowledge it so they have a frame of reference for finding it at other times. ("Do you remember how you felt when you held the soap bubble in your hand? See if you can make your whole self that soft and careful right now.")

In working with very intense and easily excitable children, you need to match their intensity without matching their loud voices and frantic movement, because that will stir them even more. You may have to work intensely to stay calm and centered.

Highly energetic children help remind us not to make dance always slow, soft, and graceful. You need to include plenty of large, vigorous movements, such as running, galloping, leaping, and jumping, as well as sudden strong movements. However, all movement needs to have structure that includes a beginning and ending, and you need to make sure that the ending comes before the children get out of control. You will quickly become sensitive as to how soon you need to end a *run* with a *freeze*. Sudden shape changes to a drum cue work especially well because they are exciting yet have the control element built in. Rhythmic accompaniment also helps to structure the movement and keep the group together. An example of an energetic but highly controlled dance structure is one I have used in a theme of a "magic garden." The weeds pop up, pull themselves out, and throw themselves away in a dance.

In addition to large, vigorous movement, energetic children need to do small movement that can help them focus. Moving small body parts, or even "making a movement so tiny I can't see it" is helpful. Taking tiny steps (and now even *tinier* ones!) also helps children control themselves.

Teaching Idea: Magic Weeds Dance

Concepts: Sudden Shape Changes; Elevations

Activity: (See story of *Magic Garden* in Appendix D.) *Dance Structure:* Children start by lying on the floor. They "pop up" suddenly into a shape when directed by the drum. Repeat four more times. Then they pull themselves off the floor into the air (a big jump) and throw themselves away (collapse limply on the floor, as softly as a wilted weed).

Teaching Note: Give the cues in a rhythmic manner, accompanied by marching music.

$\frac{4}{4}$ | pop! (f r e e z e) | Two! (f r e e z e) | Three! (f r e e z e) |

Four! (f r e e z e) | Five! (f r e e z e) | pull yourself out and |

throw yourself away | (rest and ready to begin again) |

Most disruptive children have a hard time dealing with open space in any way other than zooming through it. They may benefit from an unmovable marker (such as a piece of colored tape) on the floor to designate their spot; I also try to stay as close as possible to that spot.

In addition to children who disrupt accidentally, some children intentionally find ways to disrupt. Such a child is usually a discouraged child, one who feels that he or she can gain recognition and a sense of importance only through misbehavior. It is the one skill these children are sure that they are good at, and they usually get constant reminders of their success. The best way, then, to deal with this kind of situation is to ignore the disruptive behavior and give plenty of attention to other moments when the child is successful (even if you have to look very hard at first to find them). In the process of changing a child's conception of self, I sometimes try to foil attempts at disruptive behavior, turning them instead into inspirational ideas and thereby defining the child as helpful instead of disruptive. ("Jill is falling down. That gives me an idea; let's all add a fall at the end of our careful turn.")

Sometimes, behavior may be so disruptive to the rest of the group that it will be necessary to remove the child. This should be done very matter of factly, with absolutely no threats, ridiculing, or scolding, and with as little attention as possible (to avoid reinforcing the behavior you wish to discourage). In very difficult cases, it may be necessary to have another adult remove the child.

Depending on the severity of the problem and your total contact time with the child (whether you are a regular classroom teacher or a specialist that only teaches two half-hour sessions a week), this technique may take a long time to work. Meanwhile, you may feel that you are ignoring all of the other children and they may begin to make their needs more obvious. There are times when the best alternative may be to exclude the child from the dance session for a period of time. This is always a very difficult decision to make, and is usually fraught with guilt for new (and not-so-new) teachers, especially since the disruptive child may seem to need to dance the most. At these times, it helps to remind ourselves that we cannot solve every child's problems and that other children need us too. Once I had a very large class in which there were a few children who were unable to participate without disrupting the whole session. I met with these children for 10 minutes of very vigorous, very structured movement activity before I taught the rest of the class. This gave them an experience of success, rather than failure, at dance and, eventually, they were able to be integrated into the larger group.

You must remember that different children have different ways of disrupting, and some children choose techniques that are less obvious than others (and, therefore, are usually able to continue them longer).

Some children choose very "appealing" ways to disrupt, such as the child who must always be the leader, the one who always seems to be the "victim," the one who always says "Look at me," or even the child who cries too easily. These children, too, are finding ways to get their needs for attention and self-esteem met. You can best help them by gently but firmly refusing to respond to demands at inappropriate times, and by making sure you give them extra doses of attention and feelings of success at appropriate times.

CHILDREN WHO WITHDRAW

There are a variety of reasons that preschool children may withdraw from a group. Some reasons were discussed in Chapter 6 in the section on the nonparticipant. In addition, some children are just less social than others. Some take longer to feel safe in a new environment or a new activity. There are many ways that you can help shy children feel more comfortable in participating in dance. First of all, you need to ensure their safety by enforcing the ground rules. If other children seem to be out of control, smaller children in particular may feel very unsafe. Just being in the middle of a large group moving through space may be threatening.

It helps to think *small*. This means including small movement, using a small (soft) voice (and avoiding loud noises), and acknowledging even the smallest contributions of a quiet child. It may also mean working with children in a smaller group instead of a large one. If you cannot change the group size, allow children who are feeling overwhelmed to work on the edge of the group so that they will not feel "trapped."

Shy children may feel intimidated at first, but usually will join in eventually if you make the environment both safe and inviting. Some children, however, are more than just shy and need more from you.

For the very withdrawn child, relating to others in any activity may be difficult. When I work with such children, I start out expecting to do all of the relating, instead of expecting a child to adapt to me. Setting up a structure in which the child is expected to explore such problems as "what other parts of your body can you shake?" is not likely to be successful. A more appropriate approach is to play some music, watching for some movement response in the child (although you may need to watch unobtrusively while you dance!), and then try to be *with* the child by sharing (copying) his or her movement. The movement may gradually change as we share it; the tiny movement may become larger and the tense movement may become more relaxed.

Some children may find it easier to make a puppet, scarf, or stick "dance." If that is the case, I start out by acknowledging the movement of the object ("The scarf is waving") and gradually begin to give feedback to the child ("Your arms make it go fast").

I also try to connect in more physical ways. If a child will not take my hand, perhaps he or she will connect by taking hold of a rope, scarf, or hula hoop that I am holding.

SOME GENERAL SUGGESTIONS FOR CHILDREN WITH SPECIAL NEEDS

We usually identify children as having special needs because they are lacking certain skills and/or abilities. Looking at the movement of these children helps us recognize what they do have and what they can do, as well as what they are missing. For example, some children are very successful at tight, fast movement but do not use soft, slow movement; some are very successful at large movement but do not use much small movement. Teachers need to help all children appreciate what kinds of movement they are good at; give it a name and also your approval.

Approval is important to all of us. Such recognition is especially valuable for children whose successes are not as frequent. We need to communicate our pleasure to these children over the smallest accomplishment.

When you try to help children with special needs to expand their movement possibilities, just as when you introduce other new experiences, try to make only one change at a time. For example, if a child uses tight, fast movement, encourage tight, slow movement, or soft, fast movement, rather than trying to change both the tension and the speed at the same time. Dance therapists, and dance educators who have studied movement analysis, are specially trained in observing movement and identifying the "next step" for children to take. If a child in your preschool class is also working with one of these specialists, he or she may be willing to make suggestions regarding the movement needs of a particular child.

Dance for most of us is a therapeutic experience in some way. Dance is even used directly as a form of psychotherapy by persons with special training as dance therapists. It is important, however, that those of us who are *not* trained as therapists recognize that there are some children who need more help than we can give. We need to refer these children to places where they can get the appropriate help.

In working with children with special needs, you may feel that each child seems to need individual attention all the time. A parent-child class, or even a class that combines children with senior adults, can provide this kind of attention. The next chapter discusses how to structure such a class.

CHAPTER 9

Leading a
Parent-Child Session

More and more preschools and day care centers have been finding that their job has expanded to include not just educating and caring for children, but educating parents as well. This may include offering a lending library, sponsoring discussion groups, providing information on family-oriented community-sponsored activities, and sponsoring social occasions for the family. A more unusual kind of event, but one that could prove to be very special for parents, children, and your school, is a parent-child dance session. This means a session in which parents participate, not just for the sake of their children, but to do something for themselves and their relationship with their children as well. Activities are designed to be challenging and satisfying to both parents and children; but, rather than just providing for parallel (side-by-side) participation, they should encourage interaction, cooperation, and mutual respect and trust. The child can be the leader of the parent as frequently as the reverse.

Such a session can serve many purposes. It is a wonderful way to share with parents what you have been doing with the children without setting up a performer-audience situation. It provides a chance for parents and children to enjoy their own movement and each other in a very special way. It can set up the framework to continue this kind of interaction at home on their own, giving them a new activity to share. Finally, many parents have reported therapeutic effects in the relationship with their child following such a session.

You may be asking, "Would parents be interested in this kind of experience?" More and more adults are becoming interested in rediscovering their bodies, as shown by the increased popularity of jogging and other athletic pursuits, and activities that can integrate the whole body, including dance. Of course, many adults would be threatened by the idea of "dancing," but the actual session should not be threatening to anyone. It is important to be just as concerned with the parents' feelings in these sessions as you are with the feelings of the children. It might be helpful to call it a "movement session," initially avoiding the word *dance*. You also might wish to plan sessions in more familiar media first (such as a parent-child art class) to accustom them to the general idea.

Depending on your intent and the setting in which you will be working, a parent-child dance session could take 10 minutes as part of an Open House, with adults moving while sitting in their chairs, or could range up to a 1-hour afternoon or Saturday morning event; sections of the plan that follows could be used for minisessions. The session would ordinarily be divided into three parts: a warm-up, the body of the session, and the ending.

THE WARM-UP

Preschool children are ordinarily so active, and their muscles are so flexible, that it is not usually necessary to do separate warm-up exercises for the typical half-hour session. However, the situation is different for adults, and you should plan a warm-up to avoid strain and possible injury. The warm-up can also serve other purposes. It can be fairly directive (which can make adults feel more comfortable at first, knowing that they are not being asked to contribute anything "creative"), and it can be designed to provide a chance for the child to *help* the parent (a real role reversal for many).

For the warm-up, you should plan activities that will increase the core body temperature and allow the muscles and joints of the body to start working so they will be able to move more strenuously during the class.

Light jogging is a good way to make the body feel warm. The child can lead the parent in jogging around the room; when you give a signal, they can turn around so the parent leads the child. From this activity, it is easy to make a transition to showing the difference between just jogging and "magic running."

After everyone feels warm (which can happen fairly quickly in a warm room), you need to focus on specific body parts and joints. It may be helpful to make a list of major parts:

Head

Neck

Torso (including hips, abdomen, shoulders, and back)

Arms (and elbows)

Hands (and wrists)

Fingers (ordinarily do not need special warm-up)

Legs (and knees)

Feet (and ankles and toes)

Ordinarily, you should start in the middle, with the largest body part (torso) and work outwards toward the smaller parts at the ends. This may feel like more of an exercise period than dancing, although you may want to use music to provide a "background." However, unless you have significant understanding of the principles of safe exercise, you should probably stay away from more traditional exercises, many of which are potentially harmful.[1] Focus on gentle movement; it should *not* hurt. (Let everyone know they should stop at any time during the class if any of the movement they are doing is painful.) Easy wiggling and circling are good choices, as long as no arching of the neck or lower back is involved. Some other activities to help prepare the body for more strenuous movement are:

Mirroring. Parent and child face each other. One leads the movement, slowly enough so that the partner can stay exactly with him or her; then, reverse the leadership. (You may call out body parts for the leader to use.)

Echoing. This is like mirroring, except that the leader moves and then freezes; the follower repeats the leader's movement and then freezes. Then the leader begins again.

Painting. The child puts imaginary "paint" on a designated body part of the parent, who uses it to "paint" designs in the air. (You may tell them when it is time to put some paint on another part.)

Before you proceed further, you might suggest that the adults gently stretch out any of their muscles that feel tight.

THE BODY OF THE SESSION

After the warm-up (approximately 15 minutes in a 1-hour session), the real dancing can begin. In planning this portion of the session, you may wish to select a theme such as one you would use with the children, or you may wish to focus just on "being together," planning a series of dances for parents and children to do together. Some favorite "being together" dances in my sessions include:

A Hugging Dance. Explore hugging parts of one's own body that do not get enough attention (feet? shoulders? nose?). Then, let parent and child find different ways to hug each other. To create the dance, parent and child hug each other, then dance apart for an individual hug, and then come back together to hug each other; repeat. (Try to hug a new way each time.)

A Shape Dance. Parent and child connect to make a shape, then move apart to make their own shape, then move back together, etc. (Try to make a new shape each time.)

---

[1] An easy to understand reference on this subject is *Surviving Exercise* by Judy Alter (Boston: Houghton-Mifflin, 1983).

Hugging Dance

"Pipe Cleaner People." The parent begins sitting. The child carefully moves the parent, one part at a time, to change the parent into a new shape. Eventually reverse the roles. (Use pipe cleaners to demonstrate how a shape can be changed and then held.)

A Picture in a Frame. The parent makes a shape with negative space (the "frame"). The child enters the negative space and makes a shape. The parent moves to a new spot on the floor to make a new shape, and so on.

A Rocking Dance. The parent rocks the child in his or her arms. Then, he or she explores other ways to make a rocker for the child. After they have discovered several ways, start the dance, giving a signal periodically to change to a different way.

A Swinging Dance. Parent and child clasp hands and swing them; then, they explore other ways to swing together. In the dance, change from one way to another on signal. (Swinging music is important for this activity.)

Leading with a Magic Wand. The child touches one body part of the parent with his or her finger—the "magic wand." Using that "magic wand," the child leads the parent all about (high and low, in circles, etc.). Of course, the rest of the body will follow, but the attention is on the part that was touched. Switch to a new part on signal. (Give parents a chance to lead, too.) Use music with a real sense of movement.

A Bird Dance. This is a chance for the parent to take a rest! Each parent makes a "nest" for his or her child; the children can nestle in and then soar to a new spot in the room where they can perch (balance on one part) before returning to the nest. (Be sure to explore the qualities of the words *soar* and *perch*.)

If you watch parents and children closely, you may see *new* ideas for a "together" dance. For all of these structures, musical accompaniment and a clear beginning and ending will help them become more like dances than games. The session will probably be noisier than one with just children, but encouraging interaction is one of your goals! Do remind parents and children to be gentle with each others' bodies as well as with their own.

Also, try to be sensitive to the fact that adults may tire more easily than their children. (They will remind you!) Throughout the session, try to alternate activities that are more and less vigorous.

The use of a book as a structure for dance (as discussed in Chapter 7) can be especially helpful for adults as well as give them ideas they may use when they read to their children. Again, try to structure each activity so that parents and children will be involved *together*.

THE ENDING

The ending of the session should be a relaxation activity, for the sake of the parents as well as the children. Two favorites that have become rituals in some families are:

1.   The parent lies on the floor (abdomen down). Each child lies next to the parent and then carefully rolls over him or her, giving the parent a delightful massage in the process.

2.   The parent lies on the floor (back touching the floor). Each child carefully "checks" his or her parent by lifting the arms and legs (they should feel heavy if relaxed) and then placing them gently down. Check neck relaxation by rolling the head from side to side. Then, the children lie down and the parents check them.

Teaching Idea: Where the Wild Things Are by Maurice Sendak

1. Idea: Max gets angry

    Concept: Movement we do when angry (shapes with tightness)

    Activity: The parent runs to a spot on the floor and freezes in a shape that he or she might make when angry. The child runs to the parent and gives him or her a hug or kiss to make the shape melt. Repeat.

2. Idea: The ceiling becomes covered with vines

    Concept: Swinging (on vines)

    Activity: See the idea for a swinging dance on page 128.

3. Idea: Max sailed off in a boat

    Concept: Moving another person through space

    Activity: Each parent creates a "vehicle" to transport their child through space.

4. Idea: Wild rumpus

    Concepts: Jumping, hanging, marching (see picture in the book)

    Activities: a. Explore jumping; make a jumping dance (while tired parents play drums).
    b. Find ways the child can "hang" from the parent.
    c. Children lead a parade of parents.

PLANNING FOR SUCCESS

In planning a parent-child session, be aware that adults require more room than children, so that a space that is adequate for 20 children may seem cramped with 10 children and 10 parents. This may limit the kind of activities you will plan.

   If you are setting up a special time for a parent-child session (rather than including it as part of another event), you may wish to think about defining possible limitations. How many people can you accommodate? How many children can work with each parent? (Some families may have two or even three children at your school; it is rather difficult to get the kind of interaction you desire if there are more than two children per parent.) May older or younger siblings attend? (Older children often love the opportunity to be as physical as their younger siblings with their parents. Be aware of the age range for which activities are designed, and the possible disruptions if you have infants or toddlers present.) What about children who do not attend your school, who may be friends of other children attending? It is best to make a decision on these issues and inform parents ahead of time, rather than have hard feelings and/or a frustrating situation.

If you have been working with the ideas and suggestions in this book so far, you are very aware by now that sharing dance with children enriches not only their lives, but yours. In the most successful parent-child sessions, parents, too, come to this understanding.

Resources and Strategies for Recorded Music

There are a number of recordings made especially for children, or for dance, or even for children's dance. I have listed below some that I have found most useful in preschool dance classes. They are not, however, the only ones that may be used. In fact, you may teach very successfully without using any recordings on the following list. I list them only because they are ones you might not discover otherwise, and they are useful if you have a budget for purchasing records.

Adventures in Rhythms (Ruth White) Rhythms CC623

> Three smaller records, including an incredible variety. Mostly short bands, but extremely useful.

Come Dance with Me (Virginia Tanner) Hoctor 3078

> A *long* band of galloping rhythm is especially useful.

Dance Music for Preschool Children (Bruce King) S&R 407

> *Note:* Basic rhythms are much more useful than the variations on nursery rhymes. Piano only.

Progressions: Music for Modern Dance (Evelyn Lohoefer de Boeck) Dean Records.

> A variety in qualities and instruments make this especially useful.

Street Song (Carl Orff) Quintessence PMC-7127

> Very regular rhythms using xylophones, glockenspiels, and other percussion instruments.

All of these recordings, and many others, are available from the *Children's Book and Music Center*, P.O. Box 1130, Santa Monica, CA 90406. They have a catalogue for mail ordering.

An alternative strategy is to go through your own record or tape collection and those of your friends. Listen especially for music with the following characteristics:

> Music that moves—that makes you feel like dancing. This is the most important characteristic. Try to find music with a predominating sound that "goes somewhere" as contrasted with rock music that feels like a strong constant beat in one place. Music that is very static and quiet may be more useful for concentration activities other than dance.

> Music that has a clear quality (*strong*, or *marching*, or *delicate* for example) or sections with clear qualities.

> Instrumental (no words) or words that are less important than the quality. (Recordings by Simon and Garfunkel often fall into this category.)

> Music that uses different instruments. (All piano or all strings gets tiresome.)

I have found music with these qualities on recordings by the following artists; this is not a complete list of all possibilities:

Mark Isham

Chuck Mangione

Shadowfax

Tomita

Windham Hill

George Winston

Paul Winter

Other good sources include

1.   Folk (traditional) music from different countries.

2.   Classical music, especially that performed by soloists and small chamber ensembles. (The sound of a large symphony orchestra may overpower the movement of small children.)

You will probably never find an entire record that you will use in preschool dance classes. Most will have only one or two bands that you will find useful. While records are easier to use than tapes, most teachers cannot afford to buy records with such limited use. An alternative solution is to tape record those bands that you will use.

There are some disadvantages to using tapes instead of records. The major one is that it takes longer to find that "right place" on a tape than it does to locate the right band on a familiar record. There are, however, some strategies that will make tape recordings more functional in teaching preschoolers.

1.   Use shorter tapes rather than longer ones (so you will not have as much searching to do).

2.   Record useful bands several times consecutively on one tape.

3.   Label each tape carefully, not only with the name of the music (and the number of the counter if you have more than one piece on a tape) but with qualities and particular uses.

4.   As you plan a specific session, select the music for an activity and then cue the tape to the right starting place.

5.   Do not use more than one piece of music on a single tape in the same class.

A very useful piece of equipment is a portable tape player that will both record directly from a phonograph *and* make copies of tapes. With such equipment, having a supply of music for teaching will be made much easier.

Ideas for Use
in Lessons

A. SEASONAL

1. *September*

   New friends (body parts say "Hello")
   New faces (and discovery of other body parts)
   New responsibilities (setting up ground rules)

2. *October*

   a. Leaves

      Shapes: long and pointed, wide and flat, curled, full of holes, etc.

      Movement: hanging from one point, falling, blowing, drifting, swirling; relationship of the wind

   b. Halloween

      Magic!

      Scary shapes, scared shapes

      Ghosts: Soft bodies, floating

      Sneaking

      Making a "witches" potion (see "Magic Soup" in section B)

      Healthy treats: Popcorn (quick jumps and hops), cheese (melting), oranges (squeezing; tension, relaxation), raisins (shriveling), etc.

3. *November*

   a. Thanksgiving

      Dances about things children are thankful for (with appropriate translation into the elements of movement; may include thankfulness for body parts)

   b. Indian dances

      Dances about the "spirits" of selected growing things

      Hunting dances: Dance of the large animals (galloping, leaping, freezing, and looking for danger)

      Dance of the small animals (see text, p. 25)

      Dance of the bow and arrow (bending, then "shooting" self through space)

      Dance of the fire (pointed shapes changing suddenly)

4. *December: Christmas and Hanukkah*

   a. Magic!

   b. Elves workshop: hammering (body parts up and down), scissoring (open and close), sawing (back and forth), sewing (in the air), painting (in the air, on body parts)

   c. Cookie baking: mixing, rolling, soft shapes that become hard

   d. Toy shop story about toys that come to life and dance: puppets (body parts), balls (bouncing whole body and parts), jack-in-the-box (pop up into different shapes), inflatable toys/balloons (blow up into different shapes), soldier/robot/wind-up toys (tension, direction), rag dolls (relaxation), transformers (shape changes)

   e. Stars (stretch out body to make five "points")

      Balancing on points, "breaking" (bending) points

      Spinning stars, hopping stars, etc.

   f. Drummer boy: drumming on different body parts; finding new places in the room for drumming

5. *January*

    a. New Year's—exploding

    b. Snow and ice (see text, Chapters 4 and 5)

        Shivering (vibrating; body parts)

        Snowballs and snowmen (hard shapes that melt)

        Footprints (and body part prints)

        Icicle (long narrow shape), snowball (round shape), and snowflake (fancy shape)

        Careful walking, slipping, and falling

        Snowflakes (crystals, floating, drifting, melting, shapes with holes and points)

        Figure skating (smooth sequences of movement, floor patterns, falling)

6. *February: Valentine's Day*

    Rhythm patterns (on heart candies?)

    Floor patterns (valentine shape)

    Ways to say "I care about you" (patting, rocking, etc.)

7. *March/April*

    a. Rain

        Clouds (soft and curved)

        Lightning (zig-zag shapes, sudden changes)

        Thunder (sounds with body parts, or pushing against floor)

        Rain (tapping sounds, or runs that cover the floor)

        Rainbow (curved pathways)

        Stars (pointed shapes)

    b. Wind: Gentle blowing or strong gusting; feeling of being blown; kites (with streamers as tails?) and how they dive, dip, suspend, etc.

    c. Seeds growing into plants

Seeds (something magic—a secret—inside; finding a new spot to grow, and get there by floating like a dandelion seed, spinning like a helicopter seed, etc.)

Shoots (body part poking, pulling rest of body up)

Buds (wrapping around oneself)

Blooming (into a new shape; opening and closing like morning glories)

Being picked (by the teacher) and arranged

Wilting (hard shape turning soft)

d. Other signs of spring

Ice cracking, snow melting

Birds and butterflies, other animals

e. Planting a garden (see Magic Garden Story, Appendix D)

f. Easter

Eggs hatching (poking with different body parts, stretching, hatching into a "new" shape)

Peter Cottontail song (change the word "hopping" to a different kind of motion in each verse, so children can be "tiptoeing down the Bunny Trail," etc.)

Funny Bunny dances (if you were a Funny Bunny and didn't want to hop—)

8. *May/June*

Endings, good-byes (meeting and parting; saying good-bye with body parts)

Summer time activities (abstraction of such as mosquito slapping, etc.)

The beach
  Seashells (spirals, opening and closing)
  Waves (stretching up and falling down)
  Dolphins and whales (leaping up, "diving" under)
  Crabs (scurrying)
  Seaweed (floating)
  Jellyfish (quivering)

B. OPEN STRUCTURES THAT CAN USE PRACTICALLY ANY KIND OF MOVEMENT

1. *Magic Soup*

    Mix up magic soup in a drum or other container (real or imaginary)

    Add magic ingredients, with suggestions from children (stardust, frog's eyes?)

    Mix it, taste it . . . it's running soup, and anyone who eats it starts to run—Freeze. Continue with other kinds of motion

2. *Magic shoes*

    Wear magic shoes that become jumping shoes, slow motion shoes, etc.

3. *Traveling to a new planet*

    Travel to a bend and stretch planet, where people can do only this kind of movement

    Return to "spaceship" (circle) and travel to another planet

    Use other means of transport; by boat to a new island, by train to a new country

4. *Wishing doll* (or other object)

    Rub the doll and wish to gallop, to float, etc.

5. *Gift giving*

    Give a gift of twirling, twisting, etc.

C. SHOP STORIES

See Appendix D for story about the shape shop. Vary the story to make a toy shop, jumping bean shop, motion shop, etc.

D. OTHER THEMES

1. *Breakfast* (combine two or more of the following to make a sequence)

    Toast: pushing down and popping up

    Butter: melting

    Honey: sticking

Eggs: cracking, scrambling

Salt and pepper: shaking

Bacon: stretch out long, sizzle, shrink

Juice: squeezing, shaking

A good breakfast gives you energy to run, leap, etc.

2. *Bread making* (see Chapter 4)

Kneading: changing from floppy to stretchy

Rising

Punch down (sudden level change, or punching with different body parts)

Shaping

Baking: shape gets hard

Cooling: shape moves through the air to cool; sneak back to circle for ending

3. *Pizza*

Kneading

Rising

Rolling out flat

Sauce: slipping and sliding

Cheese: melting

Pepperoni: spinning

Anchovies: slithering

4. *Washing clothes*

Washing: floppy, tumbling

Spinning the water out

Hanging up to dry

Removal from line: dropping

Optional: starching (stiff shapes) and ironing (flattening) if children are familiar with these actions

Folding up to put away

Ending: clothes sneak away and dance a dirty dance (get different parts dirty by sliding on the floor)

OR

Get blown off line and about the room for a floating dance, and then back into the wash pile

5. *Teeth*

Shapes: pointed, straight across, rounded, zig-zag (new teeth)

Relationship: wide apart, close together, crooked or straight

Movement: wiggling, falling out, biting, chewing (with different body parts)

6. *Feelings*

Anger, sadness, excitement, loneliness, etc.

Sadness

Excitement

Loneliness

etc.

Explore in movement terms: Is it strong or light? Fast or slow? Curved or Straight?

Identify shapes and movements characteristic of each feeling

7. *Boats*

Rocking in water

Motorboat: speed, direction

Sailboat: floating

Canoe: gliding

Houseboat: relaxing

8. *Birthdays*

"Happy Birthday" song: gallop to rhythm; freeze on word "you"

Candles: shapes melting, dripping, flickering

Gifts: tie a ribbon on selected body parts for free improvisation

Parties: surprise shapes, surprise movements

9. *Circus*

   Clowns: make a crazy face, a crazy shape, do a crazy walk

   Trapeze: swinging

   Balloons: shapes expanding, floating, shrinking, exploding

   Tightrope: balancing on different body parts

   Lions: finding new ways to go through hoop

   Strong men: strong shapes

   Popcorn: curl in; make sudden elevations on signal

10. *Bubbles*

    Floating, turning, changing levels, popping

    Following bubbles with eyes (focus)

11. *Building a house*—see story in Appendix D about building a house with magic

12. *Animals* (see discussion in text, p 52)

    Frog: Follow fly with eyes (focus)
           Catch fly with tongue, other body parts (sudden movement)
           Jumping (off tables or cushions; new ways to jump)
           Swimming (new ways to swim)

    Fish: Slither in and out of spaces
           Make space for fish to swim through (negative space)
           Trick swimming

    Worm: Slithering
           Twisting into new shapes
           Curling

    Monkey: Monkey faces
             New places to sit
             Swinging

    Turtle: Hiding shapes, emerging shapes

    Swans: Beautiful shapes, beautiful movement
            Gliding
            Stretching neck, other parts

    Cat: Walking softly, sneaking
          Stretching

Watching (focus)
Pouncing, landing softly

Horses: Galloping (with direction, speed changes, etc.)

Children's Literature

BOOKS TO USE AS A FRAMEWORK FOR DANCE SESSIONS

Ancona, George. *I Feel*. New York: E.P. Dutton, 1977. Expressive photos, mostly close-ups of faces, with one word captions (angry, sad, etc.).

Arnosky, Jim. *Deer at the Brook*. New York: Lothrop, Lee & Shepard, 1986. Images: Water sparkling, fish leaping, deer playing. Very brief text for very young children.

Arnosky, Jim. *Watching Foxes*. New York: Lothrop, Lee & Shepard, 1985. A few movement images in a brief text. For very young children.

Brewer, Mary. *Wind Is Air*. Elgin, IL: The Child's World, 1975. A chance to explore in both science and dance. Verbal explanations are very simple and brief.

Broger, Achim. *The Caterpillar's Story*. New York: Scroll Press, 1973. An expansion of the caterpillar-chrysallis-butterfly story with very nice movement images. Some lengthier verbal sections may need to be paraphrased.

Brown, Margaret Wise. *A Child's Good Night Book*. New York: Harper & Row, 1986. A very gentle book describing mostly animals as they stop moving and go to sleep. A nice opportunity to work with different motions and then different shapes of resting.

Brown, Margaret Wise. *The Little Island*. New York: Doubleday, 1946. Imagery of the life on and about a small island. In many cases, there are so many images on a page that you will have to arbitrarily choose which ones to work with. There is a fairly brief dramatic episode in the middle of the book that you may prefer to just read.

Brown, Margaret Wise. *The Runaway Bunny*. New York: Harper & Row, 1942. An especially warm and loving story of a bunny and his mother. The bunny imagines different ways of running away, but the mother always thinks of ways to get him back. This book has provided the framework for some especially magical sessions with children as well as parent/child sessions.

Burningham, John. *Seasons*. Indianapolis: Bobbs-Merrill, 1969. Descriptions of the seasons of the year. Only two or three words per page, not all of them easily translated into dance, but the illustrations give additional ideas. There are so many potential ideas here that you may wish to dance about only one section (season) of the book at a time, returning to it at different times of the year.

Cameron, Ann. *The Seed*. New York: Pantheon, 1975. A seed story with more potential for dancing than most, but the movement words need to be pulled out from a lengthier text.

Carle, Eric. *I See A Song*. New York: Thomas Y. Crowell, 1973. No words, just wonderful designs that can translate into motion as well as music.

Carle, Eric. *Papa, Please Get the Moon for Me*. Natick, MA: Picture Book Studio, 1986. The adventure of a father who gets the moon for his child so she can dance with it. Can be used as preparation for dancing with a prop (a moon shape cut from cardboard and decorated by the child).

Carrick, Carol & Donald. *The Brook*. New York: Macmillan, 1967. Description of a brook in a storm, with wonderful images: "Ice fingers poke," and a brook that "spills . . . spitting and splashing and spattering." There is an opportunity for dance on every page.

Carrick, Carol & Donald. *Swamp Spring*. New York: Macmillan, 1969. A series of word pictures about a swamp in the spring that can be beautifully enhanced and extended through dance.

Coatsworth, Elizabeth. *Good Night*. New York: Macmillan, 1972. Quiet images of bedtime, with only one or two lines per page. Especially nice for parent-child class.

Cole, Sheila. *When the Tide Is Low*. New York: Lothrop, Lee & Shepard, 1985. Images of the beach—water running on the shore, clams closing and opening, crabs crawling on stiff legs, etc.

Dragonwagon, Crescent. *Will It Be Okay?* New York: Harper & Row, 1977. A very special story dealing with a child's uncertainties and her mother's sensitive reassurances. Many sections can provide a good framework for dance; some are best just read.

Dragonwagon, Crescent. *Half a Moon and One Whole Star*. New York: Macmillan, 1986. Magical movement that goes on at night while a child sleeps.

Dulaney, A. *The Butterfly*. New York: Delacorte Press, 1977. A butterfly's flight across a meadow, described in words made for a dance session.

Ets, Marie Hall. *Gilberto and the Wind*. New York: Viking Press, 1963. A perfect story for exploring through dance, about a little boy and his playmate, the wind. Many possibilities for parent/child interaction.

Ets, Marie Hall. *Play with Me*. New York: Viking Press, 1955. A little girl tries to get animals in the meadow to play with her, but they all run away. The movement of the animals can easily be translated into more abstract terms for dance. Also very exciting for dance is the special quality of stillness that she discovers at the end of the book, which brings all of the animals back to "play."

Freeman, Don. *A Rainbow of My Own.* New York: Viking Press, 1966. Good preparation for dancing with a multicolored streamer.

Freschet, Berniece. *The Web in the Grass.* New York: Charles Scribner's Sons, 1972. A nature story of a spider spinning its web. The actions of the spider and other life in the meadow present images for dance.

Garelick, May. *Sounds of a Summer Night.* New York: Young Scott Books, 1963. A book that may be used simply for sensory awareness, but there are also some wonderful images for dance: a soft breeze stirring, a firefly that sparks and flickers, a squirrel going thump-pounce-leap-bounce.

Goudey, Alice. *The Day We Saw the Sun Come Up.* New York: Charles Scribner's Sons, 1961. At the beginning of the book, there is a description of the magic of dawn with many appropriate images for dance. The latter part of the book is a more scientific discussion of the relationship between sun and earth.

Grant, Sandy. *Hey Look at Me.* Scarsdale, NY: Bradbury Press, 1973. An ABC book with action words and photographs from city life; some may be extended for dance.

Green, Marion. *The Magician Who Lived on the Mountain.* Chicago: Children's Press, 1977. A bored magician and his imaginative magic. The patterns that he uses for painting the sky are especially nice for translating into movement.

Hall, William. *Winkie's World.* Garden City, NY: Doubleday, 1958. An elaboration of the world of a 2-year-old child. The beginnings of each line tend to be more useful for dance ("the dew drops sparkle. . .") than are the specific details (". . .on the lilac leaves. . .").

Hawkinson, Lucy & John. *Birds in the Sky.* Chicago: Children's Press, 1965. Describes the motion of different kinds of birds in terms that are perfect for dance.

Hawkinson, John. *The Old Stump.* Chicago: Albert Whitman and Company, 1965. Describes animal life, mostly in movement terms, around an old stump in the forest.

Hubley, Faith. *Skydance.* New York: Harper & Row, 1981. Incredible creatures dancing to inspire both dance and visual art.

Johnston, Tony. *Five Little Foxes and the Snow.* New York: G.P. Putnam, 1977. A story of little foxes who want to play in the snow. Each of the types of play they choose can be a jumping-off point for dance.

Keats, Ezra Jack. *The Snowy Day.* New York: Viking Press, 1962. A simple story of a young boy's exploring in the snow. Many possibilities for dance, if movement is taken beyond pantomime.

Landry, Anne. *Come Dance with Me.* New York: James H. Heineman, Inc., 1964. A book and record set designed especially for dance; one of the best of this kind. Story of a floppy doll who wants to dance and learns the secret from a fairy. Music (no words) and abstract illustrations suggest rather than direct specific responses, leaving much room for individual interpretation.

Lapp, Eleanor J. *In the Morning Mist.* Chicago: Albert Whitman, 1978. The special early morning time offers mostly images of magic stillness. With some imagination, many may also be danced.

Lionni, Leo. *Swimmy.* New York: Pantheon Books, 1963. The story of an adventuresome little fish. Movement images of darting, floating, pushing (lobster), etc. Seems written just for dance, with children or parent/child sessions.

Lund, Doris Herold. *Attic of the Wind.* New York: Parents Magazine Press, 1966. Full of dancing images—leaves, snowflakes, butterflies, sparks, and more.

Lukesova, Milena. *The Little Girl and the Rain.* New York: Holt, Rinehart & Winston, 1978. Rain falling soft then hard, chasing, tapping on the window, and looking from umbrella to umbrella for a little girl. Many more images are included as animals and others respond to the rain.

Mari, Iela. *The Magic Balloon.* New York: S.G. Phillips, 1970. A story told just in pictures, of the bubble (gum) that floats away to become a balloon, then an apple suspended from a branch, then a butterfly, then a flower that gets picked and turns into an umbrella.

Martin, Bill Jr. *The Wizard.* New York: Holt, Rinehart & Winston, 1970. A wizard who performs an action word on each page ("I skip—I jump—I low—I high—") with appropriate illustrations and disappears at the end.

Marzollo, Jean. *Close Your Eyes.* New York: Dial Press, 1978. A fanciful imagination makes bedtime easier. Illustrations provide cues for movement. Especially nice for parent-child classes.

McGovern, Ann. *Black Is Beautiful.* New York: Four Winds Press, 1969. Rich images of blackness in the world, many of which are readily adaptable for dance, such as black swans gliding, a black butterfly, a train, storm clouds, etc.

McKay, Louise & George. *Marny's Ride with the Wind.* San Francisco: New Harbinger Publication, 1977. The ride of Marny with the Huffing Puffer, including such images as grass and flowers blowing low, a kite dancing in the wind, and shingles rattling.

McPhail, David. *The Dream Child.* New York: E.P. Dutton, 1985. Adventure of the dream child as she meets with a weak lion who needs to become strong, crawling creatures, and others who eventually dance together around a fire. Could also imagine and dance about other places a dream child might go.

Mizumura, Kazue. *If I Built a Village.* New York: Thomas Y. Crowell, 1971. Describes the motion of animals that might be found "along the river in the woods," in words that readily evoke dance. Descriptions clear and brief.

Mizumura, Kazue. *If I Were a Cricket.* New York: Thomas Y. Crowell, 1973. Imagining being all different animals, each of whom has a way to say "I love you." Each one has possibilities of exploring through dance.

Moncure, Jane Belk. *Fall Is Here!* Elgin, IL: The Child's World, 1975. Describes in simple verse the activities and changes of fall. Includes a child "being" the wind and the leaves. Also words and music to a song about leaves dancing.

Moncure, Jane Belk. *Winter Is Here!* Elgin, IL: The Child's World, 1975. Describes in simple verse the sights, sounds, and activities of winter. Includes a child "being" a snowflake, a snowbird, a snowball. Words and music to song at the end.

de Paola, Tomie. *When Everyone Was Fast Asleep.* New York: Holiday House, 1976. A simple but magical story of two children's encounter with the Fog Maiden.

Patterson, Diane. *If I Were a Toad.* New York: Dial Press, 1977. A child imagining he is all sorts of animals. Animal movements can be abstracted to become dance.

Quin-Harkin, Janet. *Benjamin's Balloon.* New York: Parents Magazine Press, 1978. The story of Benjamin's balloon as it gets bigger and bigger, squashing everything in his house, until it finally lifts him into the air for a floating ride about town.

Reesink, Maryke. *The Wishing Balloons.* New York: Holt, Rinehart & Winston, 1971. Magic balloons take children to the sea and other places that present dance images. May also add other imaginary places (a galloping island? a tiptoeing mountain?) where wishing balloons might take you.

Rockwell, Anne & Harlow. *Thruway.* New York: Macmillan, 1972. A very brief and simple book describing a trip on a thruway. With some imagination, can provide an interesting session dealing with such images as speed, direction, patterns (of a cloverleaf), opening and closing (of a drawbridge).

Roy, Ron. *Three Ducks Went Wandering.* New York: Seabury Press, 1979. Just a few images for dancing, making it appropriate for a shorter session. Includes soaring of a hawk, slithering of a snake (who ties himself into knots), and leaping after butterflies.

Ryan, Cheli Durán. *Hildilid's Night.* New York: Macmillan, 1971. An amusing story of an old woman's attempts to chase away the night. Many of her techniques can be translated into dance.

Ryder, Joanne. *A Wet and Sandy Day.* New York: Harper & Row, 1977. A child at the beach in sun and rain. Action words include jumping, drifting, wiggling, walking through puddles, and leaping in them.

Ryder, Joanne. *Fog in the Meadow.* New York: Harper & Row, 1979. Full of kinesthetic imagery: the wind pushing and shoving its way through the grass, the clover dancing wildly under the rabbit's nose, the spider stretching its long legs, etc.

Schertle, Alice. *My Two Feet.* New York: Lothrop, Lee & Shepard, 1985. Lots of things that two feet can do, such as dancing, running, stepping on a hot sidewalk, making footprints.

Schick, Eleanor. *City in the Summer.* New York: Macmillan, 1969. Full of movement images of a city and of the beach. Just a few lines per page.

Schweninger, Ann. *On My Way to Grandpa's.* New York: Dial Press, 1981. A child's walk in the rain, with a few good movement images, such as breeze shaking a branch and thunder rolling.

Sendak, Maurice. *Alligators All Around.* New York: Harper & Row, 1962. An alphabet book, with each letter beginning an action word, many of which can be a springboard for dance if they are taken beyond pantomime.

Sendak, Maurice. *Where the Wild Things Are.* New York: Harper & Row, 1963. Full of images that translate beautifully into dance—angry feelings, vines growing, a boat sailing, a "wild rumpus" (which need not be a free for all in your session if you work with motion evident in the illustrations: jumping, swinging, and parading). Also very adaptable for parent/child sessions.

Shulevitz, Uri. *Dawn.* New York: Farrar, Straus, and Giroux, 1974. One of my favorites for use in dance. Brief but beautiful choice of words and dreamlike illustrations enhance the sense of wonder of the early morning time. (*Hint*: Explore images of stillness and silence by first finding their opposites.)

Shulevitz, Uri. *Rain Rain Rivers*. New York: Farrar, Straus, and Giroux, 1969. Rhythmic wording and the illustrations about rain are perfect for stimulating exploration in dance.

Simon, Mina Lewiton. *Is Anyone Here?* New York: Atheneum, 1967. A poem about the secret life on the beach, under the sea, and in the sky. So full of kinesthetic images that one must be selective.

Skofield, James. *All Wet! All Wet!* New York: Harper & Row, 1984. A child's walk in the rain, with images from nature, including frantic gnats that swarm and dance, slow fish rising, deer slipping by.

Skofield, James. *Nightdances*. New York: Harper & Row, 1981. Story of a magical night when a child slips out of doors to dance with the night; he is joined by his mama and papa. Beautiful poetic text; read it through and then create your own magic dances from the images.

Skorpen, Liesel Moak. *We Were Tired of Living in a House*. New York: Coward-McCann, Inc., 1969. Four children and their pets try some unusual places to live. Each is described with vivid movement imagery.

Thomas, Ianthe. *My Street's a Morning Cool Street*. New York: Harper & Row, 1976. Describes the street of a city neighborhood in the morning from a young boy's point of view. Includes such images as "stretching dogs," "tired mamas," "water swirling."

Tresselt, Alvin. *Follow the Wind*. New York: Lothrop, Lee & Shepard. 1950. Adventure of the wind with floating kites, turning windmills, birds stretching their wings, lightning flashing, etc.

Tresselt, Alvin R. *White Snow Bright Snow*. New York: Lothrop, Lee & Shepard, 1947. An older book, full of images about snowy weather and its ending in spring.

Udry, Janice May. *The Moon-Jumpers*. New York: Harper and Brothers, 1959. A magical book about children who dance when the moon is up. You may wish to read the whole book to capture the overall mood before you begin to "take it apart" for dance activities.

VanLeeuwen, Jean. *One Day in Summer*. New York: Random House, 1969. A young boy's explorations at the beach described with images and feelings to inspire dance.

Victor, Joan Berg. *Sh-h! Listen Again*. Cleveland: World Publishing, 1969. Sound words in nature also present images of movement in relation to seasons. Also useful for sensory awareness.

Wagner, Jenny. *Aranea*. Scarsdale, NY: Bradbury Press, 1975. Story of a spider's work of art, with images of floating and swinging in the wind, crawling into a curl, and making spirals.

Walters, Marguerite. *Small Pond*. New York: E.P. Dutton, 1967. Describes the sense of magic, beauty, and adventure of a pond as the seasons change—the animal life and how children play there. Wood engravings illustrate.

Zion, Gene, & Graham, Margaret. *All Falling Down*. New York: Harper & Row, 1951. Wonderful images of different things falling (petals, water that shoots up before falling, night falling, etc.).

Zolotow, Charlotte. *Do You Know What I'll Do?* New York: Harper and Brothers, 1958. A love story between a big sister and her baby brother. Each of the gifts she imagines for him can be a jumping-off point for a special dance.

BOOKS TO SET A MOOD AND INSPIRE FEELING FOR DANCE

Arneson, D.J. *Secret Places.* New York: Holt, Rinehart & Winston, 1971. Magical places in the country for a child to play, dream, and dance.

Baylor, Byrd. *Sometimes I Dance Mountains.* New York: Charles Scribner's Sons, 1973. Photographic essay of an elementary-school-aged girl dancing in response to different images.

Bornstein, Ruth. *The Dancing Man.* New York: Seabury Press, 1978. The dancing man passes down his special shoes and his gift to a sensitive boy who longs to dance. An especially inspiring story.

Bottner, Barbara. *Myra.* New York: Macmillan, 1979. A young girl's imagination in dancing class carries her far beyond the expected.

Bryan, Ashley. *The Dancing Granny.* New York: Atheneum, 1977. A priceless story based on an Antiguan folk tale. Charming rhythm in the words and magnificent illustrations; it is hard to read without feeling yourself dancing! Longer than other books listed; may need to be shortened for 3- to 4-year-olds.

Dayton, Mona. *Earth and Sky.* New York: Harper & Row, 1969. A dialogue between earth and sky, discovering they each have something special to share.

Dragonwagon, Crescent. *When Light Turns into Night.* New York: Harper & Row, 1975. A poem evoking the magical quality of dusk. A few sections may also inspire dance activity.

Feelings, Tom, & Greenfield, Eloise. *Daydreamers.* New York: E.P. Dutton, 1981. Drawings of children daydreaming, with poetic text. Also movement images that may initiate dance session.

Himler, Ronald. *Wake Up, Jeremiah.* New York: Harper & Row, 1979. A small boy's exuberant greeting of the sun and a new day.

Hobart, Lois. *What Is a Whispery Secret?* New York: Parents Magazine Press, 1968. Captures a real sense of magical quality and awareness of the inside.

Horowitz, Elinor Lander. *When the Sky Is Like Lace.* Philadelphia: J.P. Lippincott, 1975. Describes the magical quality of a special sky.

Hurd, Edith. *The Day the Sun Danced.* New York: Harper & Row, 1965. This book describes the wonderful feeling when the sun appears after a long winter, in terms that inspire a wonderful mood for dance.

Hurd, Edith. *I Dance in My Red Pajamas.* New York: Harper & Row, 1982. A story of the special relationship between a child and her grandparents, with whom she loves to dance (loudly!) before bedtime.

Isadora, Rachel. *Max.* New York: Macmillan, 1976. A young baseball player discovers that ballet class is for boys, too.

Lionni, Leo. *Tico and the Golden Wings.* New York: Pantheon, 1964. A story emphasizing how our different experiences make us all different.

Lukesova, Milena. *Julian in the Autumn Woods*. New York: Holt, Rinehart & Winston, 1977. The story of a young boy who sees leaves and acorns dancing with berries in the woods.

Myers, Walter Dean. *The Dancers*. New York: Parents Magazine Press, 1972. When Michael goes to work with his father, a theater technician, he meets a dancer who becomes a special friend.

Rockwell, Anne. *The Dancing Stars: An Iroquois Legend*. New York: Thomas Y. Crowell, 1971. Story of seven Indian brothers who liked to dance so much they were turned into stars.

Ryder, Joanne. *The Night Flight*. New York: Macmillan, 1985. A child's dream of flying, and her adventures while on her flight.

Schick, Eleanor. *One Summer Night*. New York: Greenwillow Books, 1977. An especially inspiring story of the warm night when "Laura breathed the summer wind and felt like dancing." Her dance spreads throughout her multiethnic neighborhood until everyone, young and old, is caught up in the magic of dance.

Shannon, George. *Dance Away*. New York: Greenwillow Books, 1982. Rabbits who dance for pleasure and then to save themselves from a fox.

Zolotow, Charlotte. *If You Listen*. New York: Harper & Row, 1980. All about listening inside yourself—even to tell if someone far away loves you.

Zolotow, Charlotte. *The Storm Book*. New York: Harper and Brothers, 1952. Vivid kinesthetic imagery, although too lengthy to really follow the book in dance sessions. This could be an excellent book to set the mood for a dance session related to a rainstorm.

Zolotow, Charlotte. *The Summer Night*. New York: Harper & Row, 1974. A little girl cannot sleep on a summer night, so she and her daddy go for a special, magical walk.

BOOKS FOR SENSORY AWARENESS

Bram, Elizabeth. *One Day I Closed My Eyes and the World Disappeared*. New York: Dial Press, 1978.

Brenner, Barbara. *Faces*. New York: E.P. Dutton, 1970.

Brown, Marcia. *Listen to a Shape*. New York: Franklin Watts, 1979. Photographic essay of wonderful shapes from nature, with a poetic text.

Brown, Margaret Wise. *On Christmas Eve*. New York: Young Scott Books, 1938.

Hoban, Tana. *Look Again*. New York: Macmillan, 1971.

Kohn, Bernice. *How High Is Up?* New York: G.P. Putnam, 1971.

Miles, Betty. *A Day of Summer*. New York: Alfred A. Knopf, 1960.

O'Neill, Mary. *Hailstones & Halibut Bones—Adventures in Color*. Garden City, NY: Doubleday, 1961.

O'Neill, Mary. *Fingers Are Always Bringing Me News*. Garden City, NY: Doubleday, 1969.

Tanz, Christine. *An Egg Is to Sit On*. New York: Lothrop, Lee & Shepard, 1978. Encourages imagination—looking at things in a new way.

Zemelman, Nathan. *Walls Are to Be Walked*. New York: E.P. Dutton, 1977. Encourages taking time to see all that is there on Jimmy's three-block walk to school.

POETRY BOOKS

Collections of poetry for young children usually offer the best source. Check public libraries for older collections.

Arbuthot, Mayhill (Ed.). *Time for Poetry* (rev. ed.). Chicago: Scott, Foresman, 1961. An extensive collection.

Cole, Joanna (Ed.). *A New Treasury of Children's Poetry*. Garden City, NY: Doubleday, 1984. Section on "First Poems of Childhood" is especially useful.

Doane, Pelagie (Ed.). *A Small Child's Book of Verse*. New York: Henry Z. Walck, 1948. Filled with many old favorites.

Jacobs, Leland B. (Ed.). *Hello, Year!* Champaign, IL: Garrard Publishing Co., 1972. Poems about months, seasons, weather, and holidays that can enhance a session involving one of these themes.

Larrick, Nancy (Ed.). *Piper, Pipe That Song Again!* New York: Random House, 1965. More contemporary choices.

Lenski, Lois. *City Poems*. New York: Henry Z. Walck, 1965. Useful poems for urban children. Use selected images for dance, rather than pantomime.

McFarland, Wilma (Ed.). *For a Child: Great Poems Old and New*. Philadelphia: The Westminster Press, 1969.

Prelutsky, Jack. *Circus*. New York: Macmillan, 1974. Poems about different circus acts that could enhance a session on this theme.

Stephenson, Marjorie (Ed.). *Fives Sixes and Sevens*. London/New York: Warne, 1968. A few are useful for preschool age.

MISCELLANEOUS BOOKS

Lionni, Leo. *Pezzetino*. New York: Pantheon, 1975. A simple tale to reinforce the uniqueness of each individual.

Sorine, Stephanie Riva. *Imagine That—It's Modern Dance*. New York: Alfred A. Knopf, 1981. A picture book on modern dance with photographs of children (multiracial but all girls) making shapes.

Sorine, Stephanie Riva. *At Every Turn! It's Ballet*. New York: Alfred A. Knopf, 1981. Photographic essay of children (dancers and everyday) showing how ballet uses everyday movements.

Wallace, Ian. *Chin Chiang and the Dragon's Dance*. New York: Atheneum, 1984. A cross-cultural view of a traditional dance in Chinese culture that a child has learned from his grandfather.

Sample Original Stories

THE SHIP-SHAPE SHAPE SHOP

Once upon a time there was a shopkeeper who had a shop. It was a very unusual shop that sold only one thing: *shapes*. It had large shapes and small ones, curved shapes and pointed ones, twisted shapes and straight ones. (Include in this list whatever kinds you have explored.)

One thing the shop did *not* have was customers. Who had ever heard of a shape shop before?

Then, one day the shopkeeper had an idea: he(she) would have a big sale and put an ad in the newspaper.

The night before the sale, the shopkeeper went around to see all the shapes, to make sure that each one was in perfect condition, really "ship-shape." He(she) checked to be sure the curves were curvy, the points were pointy, and the twists were twisty. Then, the shopkeeper went to sleep for the night in his(her) apartment in the back of the store. (That way he/she could hear if there were *any* problems during the night.)

While the shopkeeper was sleeping, the shapes all came sneaking down from their shelves and, as quiet as could be, began to dance. They began shaping, changing from one shape to another. (Add any other movement cues that you wish. Continue to give cues if necessary, while children dance.)

Finally, when the first light of morning came, the shapes were so tired that they could not keep their shapes anymore. They lay all soft and relaxed on the floor.

The storekeeper came in and took one look at the shapes. Then he(she) said, "Oh, no! What shall I do? My customers will be here any minute! All that can save me now is some magic!" Then he(she) heard the first customer at the door and went to explain what had happened.

But, while the shopkeeper went to the door, some magic *did* happen. The tired shapes were filled with magic and changed back into their real shapes, just in time. The sale was a real success; the shopkeeper had many satisfied customers.

Notes

- Tell the story first, and then briefly review the story, giving time for the children to dance the parts of the shapes. Dramatize other parts of the story if you wish.

- I ordinarily take the part of the shopkeeper. Otherwise, every child will want a turn taking this part, and there won't be time to do any other dances.

- Change the story to suit your needs. It may become a magic food shop, a magic toy shop, or any other kind.

THE MAGIC GARDEN[1]

Once upon a time there was a child who wanted to dance, but could not because his legs would not work. He had to sit in a wheelchair. One day, a wishing fairy came to see him. The fairy told the boy she could not make his legs work, but she could take him to a place where he could be happy—a Magic Garden.

This garden was so magical that it dug itself up with a magic digging dance, and the child laughed. The seeds jumped into the dirt to plant themselves; one seed jumped into his lap. Raindrops danced into the garden so the child felt cool and clean. They called the sun, who did a magic rising and setting dance. Then weeds popped up, but they pulled themselves out and threw themselves away. Then, clouds came in and made scary shapes to keep the crows away, but they didn't frighten the child. They just made him feel braver than he had ever felt before.

Then, most amazing of all, plants started to grow—every kind and every shape. Each one started to dance, each in its own way. They came

---

[1]The idea for this story was borrowed from Frances H. Burnett's book *The Secret Garden*. New York: Dell, 1987.

and danced all around the child. He reached out his arms and felt their magic going inside of him.

Can you guess what happened then?

Notes

First, explore all the kinds of movement included in the story. (This may be done the day before.) Then, tell the story and dance the dances described.

1. Digging—(the action of the shovel)—push yourself down to the floor (using strength), turn yourself over, pull yourself up.

2. Seeds—jumping.

3. Raindrops—Light running.

4. Sun—Slow rising into a shape, turn to shine on the whole (garden) room, sink down.

5. Weeds—See description of dance on p. 120

6. Clouds—Changing from one scary shape to another.

7. Plants—Each person starting in own shape, then dancing in own way.

BUILDING A HOUSE WITH MAGIC[2]

Once there was a poor housebuilder who worked all day in the hot sun to build a house. He(she) did sawing, hammering, screwing in screws, and painting. He(she) was known for the very unusual houses he(she) built, with very different shapes. As soon as he(she) built a house, he(she) sold it to have enough money to buy food and materials for the next house.

He(she) had just finished building a house one day, when a big storm came and blew it down. The housebuilder was so sad he(she) sat down on a rock and cried.

While he(she) was crying, a group of elves came sneaking out and danced building dances. First, they did a sawing dance, then a hammering dance, then a turning dance to screw in the screws, and then a painting dance. As they danced, the house got rebuilt right before the housebuilder's eyes, like magic.

The housebuilder thanked the elves—not just for rebuilding the house, but for teaching him(her) about the magic of dancing. From then

---

[2]A variation of *The Elves and the Shoemaker*

on, he(she) always danced while he(she) worked, which made the work go much faster.

Notes:
Prior to the story, explore the movements; repeat the dances during the story.

1. Sawing: stretching and bending different body parts.

2. Hammering: tapping different body parts.

3. Screwing: turning different body parts.

4. Painting: making different pathways in the air.

5. The house coming together: one at a time, each child dances to the circle, making a shape that connects to (touches) another child's shape.

Sample Lesson on a Specific Movement Theme: Curved and Angular Lines

1. *Introduction:* Show pictures of curved and angular ("zig-zag lines," "lines with points") lines. Identify curved and angular lines on objects in the room.

2. *Concept:* Curved and Angular Body Shapes

   Activities:

   (a) Explore making curved and angular body shapes.

   (b) Explore changing smoothly from one curved shape to another; explore changing suddenly from one angular shape to another.

   (c) Make a dance in two parts, based on the exploration above.

3. *Concept:* Pathways in the Air

   Activities:

   (a) Ask children to draw circles in the air with a finger, then with other body parts. Then draw straight lines, then zig-zags. Do it to smooth (curved) and sharp (zig-zag) music.

   (b) Add moving through space while drawing lines, so children "fill up all the air in the room" with designs.

(c) Make a dance in two parts: Painting the air with curves, then painting the air with zig-zags and straight lines.

4. *Concept:* Pathways on the Floor

   Activities (successful in a small group of children at least age 4):

   (a) Place masking tape on the floor in a curved pathway and in an angular pathway. Explore traveling on the lines using different kinds of movement (tiptoeing, jumping, galloping, slithering, etc.).

   (b) Give each child a piece of chalk to make his or her own curved or zig-zag pathway on the sidewalk or floor. Ask each child to tell which kind it is. Explore traveling on one's own pathway.

   (c) Make a dance: Start and end in a body shape (curved or angular) that corresponds with the pathway. Share the dances with each other: view all the curved dances at once, then all the angular dances.

   (d) Have each child make a drawing or painting that goes with his or her dance, using curved or angular lines.

Suggested Resources for Further Reading

MOVEMENT FOR PRESCHOOL CHILDREN

Cherry, Clare. (1971). *Creative movement for the developing child: A nursery school handbook for non-musicians (rev. ed.).* Belmont, CA: Fearon. A collection of activities to be done to songs and jingles; some of the suggested explorations can be used in a more flexible way.

Cochran, Norman A. (1976). *Learning on the move: An activity guide for pre-school parents and teachers.* Dubuque, IA: Kendall/Hunt. A detailed movement curriculum, with suggestions for exploration. These suggestions might then be developed into dance rather than game activities.

Curtis, Sandra R. (1982). *The joy of movement in early childhood.* New York: Teachers College Press. Theoretical discussion of patterns of motor development, followed by suggested games and activities to promote development.

Jones, Barbara Stewart. (1981). *Movement themes: Topics for early childhood learning through creative movement.* Saratoga, CA: Century Twenty One Publishing. Series of lessons, including exact words for the teacher to teach 10 different concepts through creative movement.

Lynch-Fraser, Diane. (1982). *Danceplay: Creative movement for very young children.* New York: New American Library. Parent-child activities for toddlers and preschoolers. Some are acceptable for group settings.

Nelson, Esther L. (1977). *Singing & dancing games for the very young.* New York: Sterling. Fingerplays and movement games that could be used as a beginning for more creative exploration.

Sinclair, Caroline B. (1973). *Movement of the young child: Ages two to six.* Columbus, OH: Charles E. Merrill. Focus on development of basic movement patterns during this period with photographs showing more and less mature patterns of jumping, throwing, etc.

Sullivan, Molly. (1982). *Feeling strong, feeling free: Movement exploration for young children*. Washington, D.C.: National Association for the Education of Young Children. Includes many practical suggestions and activities for movement exploration with 3-4 and 5-8-year-old children.

DANCE FOR YOUNG CHILDREN

These books focus on kindergarten and/or elementary-age children. However, there are some suggested activities in each that are appropriate for preschoolers.

Barlin, Anne. (1979). *Teaching your wings to fly: The nonspecialist's guide to movement activities for young children*. Santa Monica, CA: Goodyear.

Boorman, Joyce. (1969). *Creative dance in the first three grades*. Don Mills, Ontario: Longman Canada Limited.

Fleming, Gladys Andrews. (1976). *Creative rhythmic movement: Boys and girls dancing*. Englewood Cliffs, NJ: Prentice Hall.

Fleming, Gladys Andrews (Ed.). (1981). *Children's dance*. Reston, VA: The American Alliance for Health, Physical Education, Recreation and Dance.

Joyce, Mary. (1980). *First steps in teaching creative dance to children* (2nd ed.). Palo Alto, CA: Mayfield.

Mettler, Barbara. (1976). *Creative dance in kindergarten*. Tucson: Mettler Studios.

Murray, Ruth Lovell. (1975). *Dance in elementary education* (3rd ed.). New York: Harper & Row.

Russell, Joan. (1975). *Creative movement and dance for children*. Boston: Plays.

DANCE FOR SPECIAL POPULATIONS

Canner, Norma. (1975). *. . .and a time to dance*. Boston: Plays. A warm and sensitive discussion about creative movement with mentally handicapped individuals; many beautiful photographs.

Fitt, Sally, & Riordan, Anne. (1980). *Focus on dance IX: Dance for the handicapped*. Reston, VA: The American Alliance for Health, Physical Education, Recreation and Dance. A collection of articles regarding dance with different groups with special needs.

Kinda, Crystal L. (1976). *Body awareness for exceptional children through the creative arts*. Buffalo, NY: D.O.K. Publishers. A series of lessons designed for mentally handicapped children ages 3-8.

Levete, Gina. (1982). *No handicap to dance: Creative improvisation for people with and without disabilities*. London: Souvenir Press. Includes a section on activities for ages 3-6.

Materials on creative arts (Arts, crafts, dance, drama, and music) for persons with handicapping conditions. (1977). Reston, VA: The American Alliance for

Health, Physical Education, Recreation and Dance. An extensive bibliography of materials related to the arts with special populations. Includes books, articles, films, and organizations.

Pesetsky, Sally, & Burack, Susan. (1984). *Teaching dance for the handicapped: A Curriculum Guide.* Michigan Dance Association (300 Bailey Street, Room 201, East Lansing, MI 48823). Includes 10 activity plans, some of which are appropriate for preschool children.

Sherrill, Claudine (Ed.). (1979). *Creative arts for the severely handicapped* (2nd ed.). Springfield, IL: Charles C. Thomas. Includes an introduction to the goals and approaches of the dance therapist.

MISCELLANEOUS

Cherry, Clare. (1981). *Think of something quiet: A guide for achieving serenity in early childhood classrooms.* Belmont, CA: Pitman Learning. Many suggestions for helping children find their quiet selves; includes relaxation activities.

Hendricks, Gay, & Wills, Russel. (1975). *The centering book: Awareness activities for children, parents, and teachers.* Englewood Cliffs, NJ: Prentice Hall. Many relaxation and awareness activities, some of which are appropriate for young children.

Hendricks, Gay, & Roberts, Thomas B. (1977). *The second centering book: More awareness activities for children, parents, and teachers.* Englewood Cliffs, NJ: Prentice Hall. A few of these relaxation activities are suggested for all ages.

Zirulnik, Ann, & Abeles, Jeanette (Eds.). (1985). *Resource lists for children's dance.* Michigan Dance Association (300 Bailey Street, Room 201, East Lansing, MI 48823). Sixty pages listing resources in books, records, films, and other materials for children's dance. Includes some other M.D.A. publications. *Very* valuable for new teachers.

DATE DUE

DEC 16 1996		
MAY 05 1997		
~~Res '97~~		
MR 17 '98		
MAR 4 1999		
MAY 03 2001		

Demco, Inc. 38-293